ULTIMATE
BEATLES
COLLECTION

YOUR COMPLETE GUIDE TO THE WORLD'S GREATEST BAND

Fox Chapel
PUBLISHING

©2024 by Future Publishing Limited

Articles in this issue are translated or reproduced from *The Ultimate Beatles Collection* and are the copyright of or licensed to Future Publishing Limited, a Future plc group company, UK 2022.

For more information about the Future plc group, go to http://www.futureplc.com.

ISBN 978-1-4971-0461-7

Library of Congress Control Number: 2024930457

To learn more about the other great books from Fox Chapel Publishing, or to find a retailer near you, call toll-free 800-457-9112 or visit us at *www.FoxChapelPublishing.com*.

We are always looking for talented authors. To submit an idea, please send a brief inquiry to
acquisitions@foxchapelpublishing.com.

Printed in China
First printing

ULTIMATE BEATLES COLLECTION

Introduction

Can you name any rock band that has made a bigger impact on global culture than The Beatles? With an estimated 600 million record sales—more than any other artist in history—Paul McCartney, John Lennon, George Harrison, and Ringo Starr have established a presence that cannot be outdone, no matter how big or popular your favorite current musician may be.

For that reason, we bring you the *Ultimate Beatles Collection*, a celebration of all things Beatles. Our aim with this fully comprehensive book is not just to take a look at the legendary foursome's songs, although we do that in serious detail, of course. We bring together an interconnected commentary on the revolution which the four musicians brought to art, politics, and philosophy, from their roots in the early sixties to the modern day. After all, The Beatles weren't just another band—they were a phenomenon, evolving right before their fans' eyes from a bunch of mop-tops playing rock 'n' roll covers to a powerful, transformative force, making a profound impression on the entirety of their environment.

Although John and George aren't around to celebrate the continued relevance of their band, Paul and Ringo are still out there, playing the world's biggest stages and commanding legions of fans. Beatlemania has never gone away, and we're all better off for that fact. Enjoy this chaotic, unpredictable, psychedelic ride.

JOEL McIVER

CONTENTS

THE FAB FOUR

JOHN, PAUL, GEORGE, AND RINGO

JOHN LENNON

Peacenik. Agent provocateur. Angry young man. The Beatles legend has a thousand faces, but the real John Lennon is right there in his songs.

....

In December 1970, John Lennon was asked by *Rolling Stone* magazine if he considered himself a genius. The former Beatle's reply—"If there's such a thing, I am one"—might seem conceited, but to say anything else would have been ludicrous. If the term can be applied to anyone in the pantheon, then it must surely be bestowed on the man who broke down the limits of what popular music could say and do, who wrote "Help!," "Don't Let Me Down," "Strawberry Fields Forever," "A Day in the Life," "Come Together," and all the rest.

Lennon was an easy artist to worship but a harder man to love. Born at Liverpool Maternity Hospital on October 9, 1940, the singer, by his own admission, had a cruel streak as a youth, and that fed into his Beatles career, where he was the barbed counterpoint to Paul McCartney's optimism and the author of the band's most biting songs. As his highest-profile acolyte, Noel Gallagher, pointed out, Lennon "had an edge," whether that was baiting the American Bible Belt with his claims that the band was "more popular than Jesus" or sabotaging McCartney's upbeat "Getting Better" with his gallows-humor asides. ("It can't get no worse.")

In early years, Lennon played the tough rock 'n' roller, driving The Beatles' covers-heavy sets with his pumped up, highly underrated rhythm guitar style ("I'm not very good technically," he noted, "but I can make it howl and move.") But with maturity, Lennon's musicianship developed light and shade, while his best songs became openhearted and hugely evocative, mirroring a kinder man who decried the Vietnam War and called for peace. There was the haunted piano melody and newspaper-clipping lyric of "A Day in the Life." The woozy throb of "Strawberry

"I BELIEVE IN WHAT I DO, AND I'LL SAY IT."

JOHN LENNON

LEFT Lennon as a boy, pictured at age nine with his mother, Julia Lennon.

ABOVE "If being an egomaniac means I believe in what I do and in my art or music, then in that respect you can call me that . . . I believe in what I do, and I'll say it."

Fields Forever," nodding to a childhood when Lennon already knew he was "different." The retooled Mississippi blues of "Come Together." The mind-expanding "Tomorrow Never Knows."

With the arguable exception of "Imagine," Lennon's post-Beatles output couldn't quite reach those heights—but perhaps it might have done were it not for the shocking incident of

December 8, 1980, when the songwriter was gunned down in New York at age 40. But even death couldn't snuff out his legend. Lennon still looms over every aspirant songwriter, stares from every student wall, and is cited by every artist who matters. "Genius" is the only word that doesn't fall short.

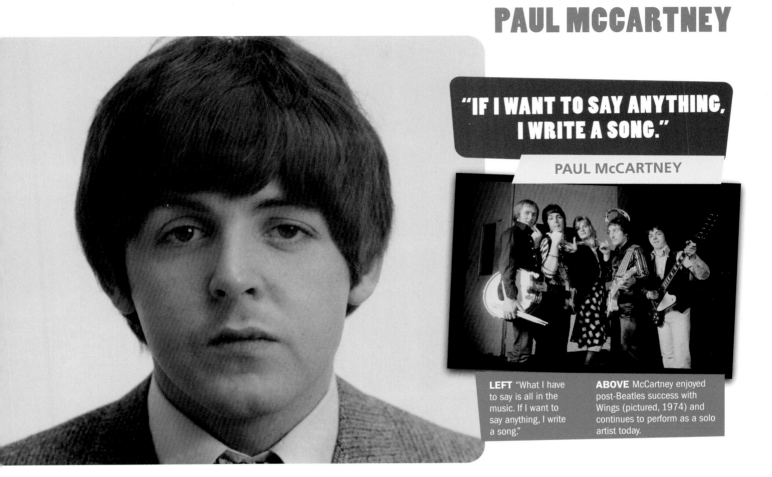

PAUL McCARTNEY

"IF I WANT TO SAY ANYTHING, I WRITE A SONG."

PAUL McCARTNEY

LEFT "What I have to say is all in the music. If I want to say anything, I write a song."

ABOVE McCartney enjoyed post-Beatles success with Wings (pictured, 1974) and continues to perform as a solo artist today.

Songwriting god, sixties survivor, and spokesman for the greatest band on Earth, Paul McCartney has spent half a century as a man on the run.

The most backhanded compliment in rock 'n' roll is that Paul McCartney was the "cuddly Beatle." Put it down to the puppyish good looks of his youth, the avuncular thumbs-up image of his later years, or the mere fact that he survived the ride, but the Beatles bassist has sometimes labored under his portrayal as less artsy or edgy than his late songwriting partner, John Lennon. In reality, even a cursory glance at McCartney's catalogue and Beatles career sinks this theory.

The bassist balanced his amenable nature with a fearless appetite for musical revolution, slashing and burning pop's conventional wisdom. Nobody has pushed the envelope further for longer.

McCartney was born in Liverpool on June 18, 1942, but he was forged in the white heat of his partnership with Lennon, after a note-perfect rendition of Eddie Cochran's "Twenty Flight Rock" secured his spot in The Quarrymen. As The Beatles set out, the pair discovered a rare songwriting chemistry—early cuts were penned "eyeball to eyeball"—but it ultimately proved too combustible, sending them into their own creative spheres (albeit with each writer often inviting the other to fix his song's holes). And it was here that McCartney thrived, his peerless melodic instincts free to swoop and soar, though always anchored by the brown thrub of his favorite Hofner violin bass.

The king of sixties London, McCartney was the fulcrum that linked all the great bands of the era: he was tight with everyone from The Rolling Stones to The Byrds. Yet the bassist was competitive too; some of his best songs were spurred by the desire to outdo Lennon ("Penny Lane" was his answer to "Strawberry Fields Forever") and Brian Wilson of The Beach Boys (the bassist took *Pet Sounds* as his cue to pull out all the stops with *Sgt. Pepper*). And when McCartney was firing on all cylinders, there was nobody to touch him. Fans fiercely respect Lennon's "A Day in the Life," of course, but it's "Let It Be" and "Hey Jude" that they sing until their throats are raw.

Wilson once noted that McCartney "has so much music in him, it seems like he never runs out of ideas," and so it proved, across a massively prolific post-Beatles career whose peaks—like 1973's *Band on the Run* and 1997's *Flaming Pie*—nudged the brilliance of the Fab Four. Now approaching his eighties, McCartney's status as the world's greatest living songwriter, bar none, is secure.

Words Henry Yates. Images Mark and Colleen Hayward/Redferns/Getty Images (Lennon & McCartney main); Icon and Image/
Getty Images (Julia Lennon); Michael Putland/Getty Images (Wings)

GEORGE HARRISON

The Beatles guitarist was a quiet revolutionary and forced his way into the spotlight with some of the band's most perfect songs.

. . . .

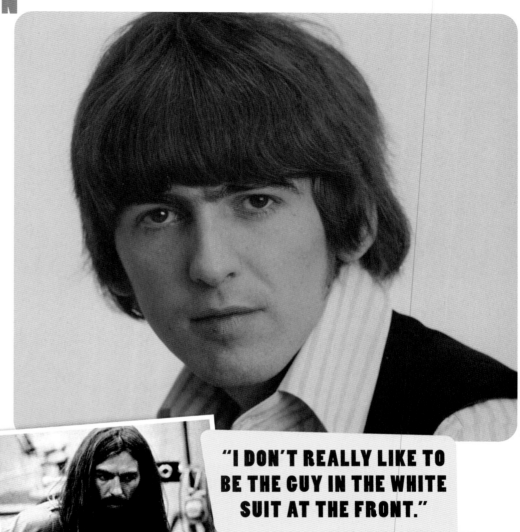

In any other band, George Harrison would have been the main event. A master guitarist with poster-boy looks. An accomplished singer whose cultural antennae was receiving everything from the wisdom of Hare Krishna to the sitar playing of Ravi Shankar. A songwriter capable of cutting diamonds like "Something," "Taxman," "While My Guitar Gently Weeps," and "Here Comes the Sun." Some felt it was the guitarist's great misfortune to be in a band alongside two principals of the stature of Lennon and McCartney—but Harrison seemed content to operate as the ultimate second fiddle. As modern rock god Dave Grohl put it, "He was the secret weapon."

On February 6, 1958, when Harrison joined The Quarrymen on the strength of his chord knowledge and a virtuoso rendition of Bill Justis' R&B hit "Raunchy," it seemed the role of this bus driver's son would be to decorate Lennon and McCartney's songs with his instrumental flair. This he did superbly on the band's early sides: revisit his leads from *Please Please Me* and *With The Beatles* or the thrilling clang of his 12-string Rickenbacker at the start of "A Hard Day's Night."

But it was during the filming of 1965's *Help!* that Harrison became far more than a foil, playing sitar for the first time, pursuing it into cuts like "Within You Without You" and challenging his bandmates to push the envelope beyond their formative jangle-pop. For all that, it's the guitarist's simplest moments that resonate. The trilling folk of "Here Comes the Sun." The choppy strut of "Taxman." The supple string-bends of *Abbey Road*'s "Something"—a song toasted by Frank Sinatra as "the greatest love song of the past 50 years" but mistakenly attributed by the crooner to Lennon-McCartney.

"I DON'T REALLY LIKE TO BE THE GUY IN THE WHITE SUIT AT THE FRONT."

GEORGE HARRISON

LEFT George was the first solo Beatle to have both a #1 single ("My Sweet Lord") and album (*All Things Must Pass*).

ABOVE "I had no ambition when I was a kid other than to play guitar and get in a ^lrock 'n' roll band. I don't really like to be the guy in the white suit at the front."

The Beatles' split barely broke his stride. Out of the blocks, Harrison's 1970 solo album *All Things Must Pass* was widely deemed the best of the post-Fab projects, while he was the impetus behind the following year's altruistic Concert for Bangladesh. Later, the guitarist was a vital cog in The Traveling Wilburys and even mobilized the cream of British cinema, having founded HandMade Films to bail out *Monty Python* and fund 1979's *The Life of Brian*.

Even when misfortune came calling—when he was stabbed by an intruder in 1999, and later when he succumbed to lung cancer in the post-millennium—Harrison bore it with his usual stoicism. "He never flinched," said the guitarist's son, Dhani. "He never felt sorry for himself. He never lost his sense of humor."

RINGO STARR

"MY SOUL IS THAT OF A DRUMMER."

RINGO STARR

LEFT "First and foremost, I'm a drummer . . . My soul is that of a drummer . . . I didn't do it to become rich and famous, I did it because it was the love of my life."

ABOVE Ringo continues to tour with his supergroup, the All-Starr Band, which first formed in 1989.

Far from a spare part, the drummer was The Beatles' blue-collar hero and underrated engine room.

••••••••••••••••••••••••••••••

It's easy to dismiss Ringo Starr as the passenger in the Beatles lineup. His original songs were infrequent and mostly forgettable. His vocal performances were reserved for the band's most frivolous and throwaway moments. Even his drum skills were negligible—at least according to John Lennon's apocryphal response when asked by a journalist if Starr was the best drummer in the world ("He's not even the best drummer in The Beatles"), something many believe he didn't say.

It's true that The Beatles might still have functioned without Starr in a way they patently couldn't if any of the other three members were removed. But Ringo was about more than just music. He was the wit-and-grit presence that kept the band tied to the streets as their lives threatened to float away from reality, the blue-collar boy-done-good who was emblematic of the rock 'n' roll dream and an eternally underrated musician who always knew exactly what the material demanded. "I've always believed," he once said, "that the drummer is there not to interrupt the song."

Born on July 7, 1940, in the tough inner-city environs of Dingle, Liverpool, Richard Starkey's musical talent was only unlocked after a teenage bout of tuberculosis. ("A woman came to the hospital with instruments," he told *Mojo*. "Tambourines, maracas, snare drums—that's where it all started.")

A month after being presented with his first kit, he hit the local circuit in outfits like Rory Storm and The Hurricanes, but it was slipping onto The Beatles' drumstool vacated by Pete Best that changed everything, both for Starkey—now Starr—and drummers that followed. Where once the drummer had been an invisible pace-setter, Starr insisted on being front and center. "The reason I had a drum riser and also the smallest kit," he said, "was I was going to make damn sure you could see me."

And whatever Lennon might have said, Starr was a far more talented sticksman than the old jokes suggested, every bit as perfect for his band as Keith Moon in The Who or John Bonham in Led Zeppelin. True, his post-Beatles career is largely kept afloat by goodwill, but his greatest moments echo through the ages. Take the thrilling solo from "The End," the propulsive tom roll that opens "She Loves You" or, above all, the languorous fills on "'A Day in the Life." "You could take a great drummer now and say, 'I want it like that,'" noted fellow drummer Phil Collins, "and they wouldn't know what to do. I think Ringo's vastly underrated."

Words Henry Yates. Images Mark and Colleen Hayward/Redferns/Getty (Harrison & Starr main); GAB Archive/Getty (George inset); Denise Truscello/Getty (All Starr Band)

Manager Brian Epstein encouraged the band to ditch their jeans and leather jackets in favor of suits for a more professional look.

MEET THE BEATLES

Imagine the scene. It's 1962, and you're seeing these four faces for the very first time. Get used to it—they're going to be around a lot.

From left to right, meet Paul McCartney (vocals and bass), John Lennon (vocals and guitar), George Harrison (vocals and guitar), and Richard "Ringo Starr" Starkey (vocals and drums). They're pictured here as young men on the very cusp of stardom,

at the ages of 19 to 22, with everything to fight for.

Little did The Beatles know at this stage that they would have become the biggest selling and most influential band ever formed, within four years of this photo being taken. In early 1963, a series of hit singles and albums would propel them into the limelight in their home country and abroad, kick-starting a wave

of successful homegrown groups dubbed the "British Invasion." By the mid-sixties, The Beatles' exploration of political and social commentary, experimentations with spirituality and alternative ways of thought, as well as innovations in making music and art would make them the primary cause of cultural change within their era. Not bad for four working-class lads from Liverpool.

THE EARLY YEARS

How the biggest band in the world started life—as a bunch of Merseyside schoolkids with a love of American rock 'n' roll.

· · · · · · · · · · · · · · · ·

The Silver Beatles: Sutcliffe, Lennon, McCartney, and Harrison on stage in 1960 with drummer Johnny "Hutch" Hutchinson, who was sitting in that day.

TOP George, John, and Paul standing outside the McCartney family home in Liverpool, circa 1960.

ABOVE A Grundig reel-to-reel tape recorder, EMI tape, and the program of performances from the Woolton Parish Church fête on July 6, 1957, where Lennon first met McCartney.

The story of The Beatles reads like a tale from an England long gone—or at least, partly so. The saga's early reference points of grammar schools, hire-purchase guitars from the little shop down the lane, summer fêtes, and 78-rpm singles made of fragile shellac sound from 70 years into the future like something out of a classical fable.

However far-off those days may be, it is a fact that today the legacy of The Beatles, the biggest rock band there has ever been or will ever be, is not only intact, it is growing. The two surviving members of the band, singer/bassist Paul McCartney and drummer Ringo Starr, both knights of the realm, are as culturally relevant—and, perhaps more significantly, as commercially successful—as they ever were.

McCartney is 81, Starr an energetic 83 (at the date of publication), and although homicide and cancer took their late colleagues John Lennon and George Harrison at a premature 40 and 58 respectively, the music the four musicians made together has a very real whiff of immortality about it. Their catalogue of songs is vast—229 is the official number they wrote as The Beatles, but co-writes, uncredited compositions, side projects, multimedia works, and their solo careers add hundreds more—and of the dozens of songs that were hits, each has a cultural significance that shows no sign of going away.

These statistics lend a fascinating contrast to the innocent, although bittersweet, story of the group's early years. The often-told tale goes as follows: Paul McCartney was born in Walton in Liverpool on June 18, 1942, and met George Harrison in 1954 at the Liverpool Institute, a grammar school. Harrison, born on February 25, 1943, was

not yet a musician, but the two bonded over the then-new American rock 'n' roll music that was flooding Liverpool and the UK. Both teenagers soon began playing music of their own, with Harrison taking up the guitar and McCartney working his way through piano and trumpet, before also settling on the six-string guitar.

In parallel, John Lennon—born on October 9, 1940—was playing in a skiffle band called The Quarrymen by late 1956. Lennon, the group's leader, sang and played guitar, and the initially fluid lineup eventually settled to include a tea-chest bassist Len Garry, a washboard player named Pete Shotton, drummer Colin Hanton, and banjo player Rod Davis. Another early member, Nigel Walley, became the group's manager and secured local gigs.

A crucial moment—not only for The Quarrymen or for The Beatles, but for decades' worth of popular music to come—was on July 6, 1957, when the group played at the St. Peter's Church Rose Queen garden fête in Woolton. Their set took place on the back of a moving flatbed lorry as part of a procession of floats containing Guides, Scouts, and Cubs and other youth groups—with the main act a display by a pack of police dogs. And so history was made.

McCartney was at that gig and was introduced to Lennon after The Quarrymen's set by their former bassist, Ivan Vaughan. Lennon was impressed enough with the younger boy's ad hoc rendition of a couple of rock 'n' roll songs to invite him to join. McCartney wisely accepted the invitation, although with the condition that he could attend Scout camp in Derbyshire and then enjoy a family holiday at Butlins first. ➨

Words: Joel McIver. Images: Keystone/Hulton Archive/Getty Images (McCartney family home); Mark and Colleen Hayward/Redferns/Getty Images (main recorder); Michael Ochs Archive/Getty Images (The Silver Beatles); Mondadori via Getty Images (main)

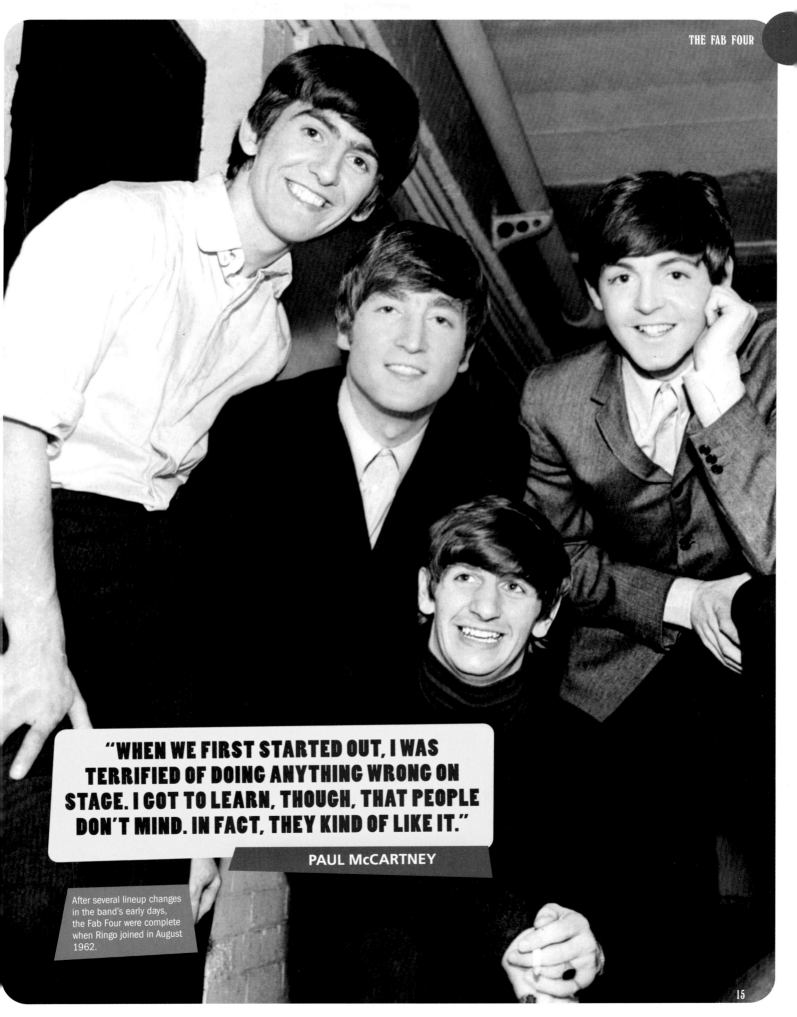

"WHEN WE FIRST STARTED OUT, I WAS TERRIFIED OF DOING ANYTHING WRONG ON STAGE. I GOT TO LEARN, THOUGH, THAT PEOPLE DON'T MIND. IN FACT, THEY KIND OF LIKE IT."

PAUL McCARTNEY

After several lineup changes in the band's early days, the Fab Four were complete when Ringo joined in August 1962.

LEFT A view of the famous Star-Club (1962-69) in Hamburg, which hosted some of music's biggest names during its time.

BELOW A childhood photo of a young George Harrison playing the guitar at his home in Liverpool.

> ## "IT WAS BEAT AND BEETLES AND WHEN YOU SAID IT, PEOPLE THOUGHT OF CRAWLY THINGS, AND WHEN YOU READ IT, IT WAS BEAT MUSIC."
>
> **JOHN LENNON**

Once he was installed as a Quarryman, the new lineup—now Lennon, McCartney, Griffiths, Garry, and Hanton—embarked on a run of rehearsals that led to local gigs in the autumn of '57. Their songs included the Everly Brothers' "Bye Bye Love" and Elvis Presley's "All Shook Up," as well as original songs, two of which included Lennon's "Hello Little Girl" and McCartney's "I Lost My Little Girl."

It's possible that the theme of early songs such as these reflected the loss of both boys' mothers: in 1956, Mary McCartney had died after surgery for cancer, while Julia Lennon would die two years later after a car struck her while she was crossing a Liverpool street. Tragedy, sadness, and a certain sarcastic attitude to the vagaries of life certainly permeated The Beatles' later work as deeply as comedy, exhilaration, and more positive emotions.

The revolving door of Quarrymen members continued to spin, with Harrison—still only 14, but rapidly becoming something of a hotshot guitarist—auditioning in March 1958 with a rendition of "Guitar Boogie Shuffle." Lennon is said to have been reluctant to invite the kid, three years his junior, on board, but McCartney was in favor and so Harrison signed up, along with a fourth guitarist, John Duff Lowe. Lennon and McCartney wanted Griffiths to switch to bass, then the most unpopular instrument in any rock band, and when he refused, they asked manager Walley to fire him. Walley himself departed soon after, and Garry contracted tubercular meningitis and stepped down.

The sole recorded evidence of the Lennon and McCartney incarnation of the Quarrymen

was a two-track single recorded on July 12, 1958, at Phillips' Sound Recording Services in Liverpool. The two songs—a McCartney/Harrison original called "In Spite of All the Danger" and a cover of Buddy Holly's "That'll Be the Day"—were recorded direct to vinyl via a single microphone. McCartney now owns this single, said by record-collecting enthusiasts to be the most valuable piece of vinyl ever manufactured.

As 1958 passed, The Quarrymen found themselves short of both members and gigs. Hanton and Lowe quit, and McCartney and Harrison played with a Welsh skiffle group called The Vikings. The group tried to rebrand, changing its name to Johnny & The Moondogs and then to the curious Japage 3, a combination of letters from their names. However, the seeds of The Beatles we now recognize were sown when Harrison took matters into his own hands, inviting guitarist Ken Brown and drummer Pete Best from the Les Stewart Quartet—with whom he had played on a break from the Quarrymen—to join him, Lennon, and McCartney in a new lineup in 1959.

By early 1960, Brown's spot had been taken by Lennon's fellow art-school student Stuart Sutcliffe, who took up the bass guitar, although he never really mastered the instrument. A

recording, "One After 909," was made, as was a rehearsal tape, but by now the band were eager to find a new identity and looked to the then-hip "beat" music label for inspiration. They came close with "The Beatals" and then "The Silver Beetles," but finally hit the bullseye with "The Beatles" in August that year. It's funny to think, all these years later, that the biggest band of all time based their name on a fairly weak pun.

At this point the group was essentially John Lennon plus backing musicians McCartney, Harrison, Sutcliffe, and Best. He was older, more experienced, and also pretty good with a devastating put-down, which ensured that the others followed his lead. This made him the focal point in 1960 and '61 when The Beatles finally hit their stride with a sequence of long and raucous shows, first at Liverpool's Cavern Club and at the Star-Club in Hamburg, Germany. They delivered over 300 gigs at the former venue, with McCartney—now the bass player, Sutcliffe having quit—anchoring the young band.

As for their shows at the Star-Club, where they performed two residencies, it must be remembered that traveling to Germany to play a show was not the relatively easy task that it would be today. Residents of Liverpool in 1960 had little idea what life was really like in ➡

ABOVE The Beatles, with original drummer Pete Best (right), perform in a Liverpool club prior to signing their first recording contract.

BELOW En route to Hamburg at the Arnhem War Memorial in the Netherlands, 1960, L-R: manager Allan Williams, his wife Beryl, Williams' business partner and Calypso singer Lord Woodbine, Sutcliffe, McCartney, Harrison, and Best.

mainland Europe, where you had to know the local language to be understood, where the food was unfamiliar, and the local culture was both mysterious and threatening. This last adjective applied particularly to Hamburg, a tough city that still bore the scars of the Second World War, which had ceased just 15 years before.

Perhaps as a result, the Star-Club shows—at which point The Beatles were aged only 17 to 20—marked the point in the story where they toughened up and transitioned towards manhood. Required to play gigs that lasted several hours, the musicians fortified themselves with Preludin, a cheap form of amphetamine, and immersed themselves in the Hamburg underground of girls and all-night partying.

Professionally, things started to really move for The Beatles when the singer Tony Sheridan recruited them as his backing band on his version of the traditional "My Bonnie." They took the name the "Beat Brothers" for the recording, and although the song is competent rather than dazzling, its real significance lies in the fact that it led the group to a meeting with Brian Epstein, whose family owned a record shop in Liverpool called NEMS. Epstein agreed

to become the band's manager in early 1962, and one of his first jobs was to tell Pete Best that he was being replaced by sometime Rory Storm drummer Ringo Starr.

The old man of the band at the ripe old age of 22, having been born on July 7, 1940, Richard Starkey had adopted his flashier stage name of Ringo Starr in 1959, even dubbing his on-stage drum solo with Rory Storm "Starr Time." He proved to be a perfect fit for the band, with his economical playing rightly taking a back seat to the singers' melodies. Best, meanwhile, gained the depressing honor of being the musician who missed out on the biggest gig in history,

given that The Beatles' profile went stratospheric mere months after he was given the boot. Best has flitted in and out of the music industry over the decades, notably fronting his own Pete Best Band in 1988, to moderate success.

By late 1962, the die was truly cast for The Beatles, with a manager, a record deal courtesy of the Parlophone label, and a lineup that was both competent and experienced. All they needed now was a hit single to kickstart their career. Lennon and McCartney put their heads together and pondered possible titles. Perhaps something with the word "love" in it would be a good idea, they thought.

THE CAVERN CLUB

Before fame came calling, The Beatles played almost 300 engagements at The Cavern Club in Liverpool, a brick cellar that was regularly packed with faithful—and at that stage, strictly loyal—fans. The group's drummer at the time was Pete Best, a competent if unspectacular sticksman who did a serviceable job of backing the other three musicians' rock 'n' roll

extravagances; however, he was replaced in 1962 by Ringo Starr, himself something of a legend on the Liverpool circuit for his showmanship.

Although this photo shows the youthful musicians in full flow, it doesn't reveal the considerable power of The Beatles at this early stage in their careers. Playing sets that lasted hours, fueled by cheap speed

substitutes, and honing their skills for their future endeavors, the band looks friendly here—but they wouldn't hesitate to tangle with hecklers if necessary. We're also spared the sight of sweat running down the walls, and the pint glasses of urine that stacked up near the stage because the club was too tightly packed for audience members to visit the bathrooms.

GEORGE, Paul, Pete Best, and John on stage at The Cavern Club in February 1961.

THE FIFTH BEATLE

The key individuals in the Fab Four's orbit who have all, at some time or other, been dubbed "the fifth Beatle."

S ift through any biography of The Beatles and the chances are that at some point there will be a reference to "the fifth Beatle." It's a phrase first coined by the media at the advent of Beatlemania in late 1963, and it's one that over six decades on shows little sign of waning.

The fifth Beatle refers to any individual whose skills were pivotal to the band's trajectory, someone who was trusted and attuned to the band's sensibilities, their ambitions, or John Lennon's sometimes-caustic comments and their idiosyncratic wit. In the course of the band's eight-year existence and beyond, there are a number of key people who have been referred to as the fifth Beatle. Here are the main contenders for the title. ➡

The band pose with producer George Martin, holding their first silver disc awarded for "Please Please Me."

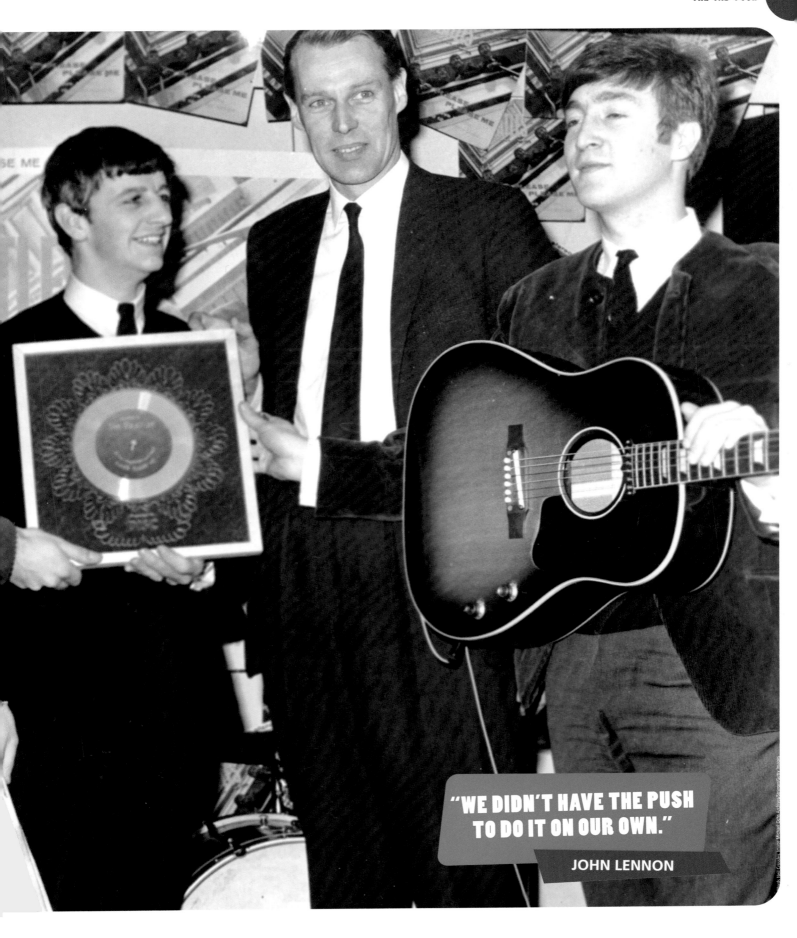

"WE DIDN'T HAVE THE PUSH TO DO IT ON OUR OWN."

JOHN LENNON

STUART SUTCLIFFE

Sutcliffe was there from the very beginning. It was he and Lennon who came up with the name "The Beatles" in Lennon's flat at Gambier Terrace in early 1960. A prodigiously talented painter, he was less gifted on bass than on canvas, but Lennon wanted him in the band so he stuck at it.

Sutcliffe was the most striking-looking member, a fact not lost on photographer Astrid Kirchherr. She and Sutcliffe became engaged and he left The Beatles in 1961 to enroll at art school in Hamburg. But on April 10, 1962, Sutcliffe collapsed and died from a brain hemorrhage. He was just 21 years old. His close bond with Lennon and his seminal influence on the band have prompted many to refer to him as the fifth Beatle.

BRIAN EPSTEIN

"If anyone was the fifth Beatle it was Brian," said Paul McCartney in 1997, and there seems little doubt that, without the charm, vision, and all-round business acumen of their impeccably attired manager, the band would have floundered in obscurity. "If he hadn't gone to London . . . from place to place with the tapes under his arm, we would never have made it," said John Lennon. "We didn't have the push to do it on our own."

Epstein worked relentlessly to get the band signed, and then transformed them into a global phenomenon. Socially and culturally, the manager and his four charges were lightyears apart, but his business was respected in Liverpool, and there was a mutual respect and trust.

"Brian was class," recalled McCartney in Ron Howard's 2016 documentary *The Beatles: Eight Days A Week*. "He was Liverpool class. In the early days it was clear he had a vision of us that was beyond the vision that we had of ourselves."

GEORGE MARTIN

The gifted producer and arranger who helped The Beatles to realize their creative visions was largely underwhelmed by the band at their first recording session in Abbey Road Studios on June 6, 1962. But he was impressed by their wit. When he asked the band if there was anything they didn't like, George Harrison replied, "Well, there's your tie, for a start." So began one of the music industry's most fruitful creative alliances ever.

While McCartney had referred to Epstein as the fifth Beatle in 1997, he clearly felt George Martin merited the title too. "He guided the career of The Beatles with such skill and good humor," he wrote in a tribute in The Guardian following the death of Martin in 2016. "If anyone earned the title of the fifth Beatle it was George."

Aspinall (right) standing in for a bedridden Harrison during a rehearsal for a TV performance in 1964.

NEIL ASPINALL

At The Beatles' 1988 induction into the Rock and Roll Hall of Fame, George Harrison said there were only two "fifth Beatles"—their public relations manager Derek Taylor and the band's road manager-turned-executive, Neil Aspinall.

Aspinall started working as the band's road manager in the early sixties, driving them around the UK in his Commer van before becoming their tour manager. In 1968, following the death of Brian Epstein, Aspinall—who had trained as an accountant—was appointed head of Apple Corps, a role he continued until his retirement in 2007, a year before his death. The appointment of Aspinall was an astute one, and McCartney praised him particularly for having the foresight to trademark the Apple name worldwide.

DEREK TAYLOR

Calm, authoritative, and effortlessly cool, The Beatles' press officer Derek Taylor brought a sense of order and dignity to the chaos that surrounded the world's biggest band.

Wirral-born Taylor was the press officer on their US concert tour in summer 1964, but left following a fight with Brian Epstein. In 1965 he moved to California, where he worked for The Byrds and The Beach Boys. In April 1968, at George Harrison's request, he returned to the UK to work as press officer for the band's newly founded Apple Corps. Taylor left in 1970 but returned two decades later as head of marketing for Apple Corps. A highly respected industry figure, he was, as one writer put it, "one of the very few men to perfect the art of saying 'no' graciously."

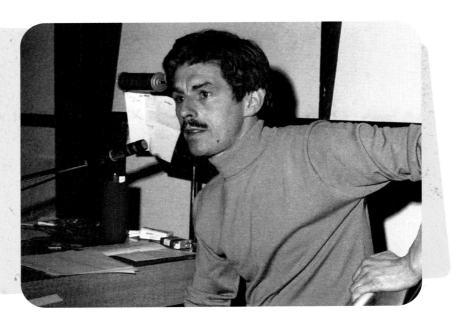

Best, second from left, was replaced by Ringo in 1962.

PETE BEST

Poor Pete Best, turfed out of the nascent band and then forced to watch as they became one of the biggest cultural phenomenons that the world has ever seen. It was producer George Martin who first highlighted his perceived shortfalls as a drummer, although it seems he was always on borrowed time from the band's perspective anyway. "We were always going to dump him when we found a decent drummer," said Lennon in a 1974 interview, although they left it to manager Brian Epstein to break the news to Best. "He said, 'The boys want you out and Ringo in,'" recalled Best. "It was a complete bombshell. I was stunned." Following his shocking removal from the band, Best went on to form his own, The Pete Best Four. After a 20-year career in the civil service he returned to music, forming The Pete Best Band in 1988.

BEATLEMANIA

PLEASE PLEASE ME

Released March 22, 1963

How does the Beatles' cheerful-but-naïve debut album stand up after nearly 60 years?

SIDE ONE

1 I Saw Her Standing There

Rock 'n' roll genius in its simplicity, "I Saw Her Standing There" is one of the finest songs in The Beatles' early canon, before irony, political commentary, and drugs—that is to say, drugs that didn't come out of asthma inhalers—were even thought of. It's virtually impossible not to tap a foot to it, even all these years later. Sure, the song is simple, even naïve, by today's standards, but luckily those are not the same standards we're using to judge it. After all, cast your mind back to the adult public's conservatism when it came to abrasive, shrieked vocals like the ones on this song, not to mention the primitive recording technology of the day, and you'll quickly realize what a miracle it is that the track was written at all.

2 Misery

John Lennon and Paul McCartney were surely rock 'n' roll's greatest salesmen, now that we look back on these early days. Take "Misery," for example, which was written with the intention of passing it onto the then-wunderkind Helen Shapiro. This slight song of adolescent angst, featuring the prerequisite Chuck Berry-indebted guitar licks and throaty vocals, comes replete with a droll sense of humor and would have been perfect teen fodder for Miss Shapiro. All that said, the vocal harmonies in The Beatles' version make the song, and thus the two-lead-singer approach—perhaps the secret sauce in the early catalogue, with hindsight—make this enjoyable song what it is, along with some funky little piano fills.

3 Anna (Go to Him)

The Beatles' arrangement of the more ambitious Arthur Alexander original doesn't quite live up to Alexander's rendition, with Lennon, in particular, struggling to equal the original vocal performance. Consider the end result as akin to The Beatles' up-

and-coming rivals The Rolling Stones' pale imitation of Alexander's "You'd Better Move On." Still, that doesn't mean there aren't some pleasures to be had here, namely the lovely "aahs" in the background and Ringo Starr's subtle fills here and there.

4 Chains

Of the cover songs here, and there are several, this take on The Cookies' original is distinctly lacking in vitality. What's more, the Beatles themselves don't appear to be that motivated by the song. They chug through it, with McCartney delivering an almost knowingly boring country and western bass part. Perhaps they'd had a hard night the night before the session.

5 Boys

Forget what we just said—this cover of The Shirelles' 1960 hit is unmissable. With its splendid intro and stop-start main riff, "Boys" owes everything to its adrenalized arrangement, climbing a plateau in the first few bars and staying there until the end of the song. The backing vocals are slick: "Bop shoo-wop, a bop bop shoo-wop!" observe Lennon and McCartney expertly as Ringo Starr delivers a rare lead vocal. Anyone who is tempted to dismiss Starr as a singer, perhaps because of his later, rather humdrum performances on "Octopus's Garden" and "Yellow Submarine," should check out his vocal delivery here—he lays on the full rock 'n' roll performance, adding whoops and yells with great abandon.

6 Ask Me Why

This slightly forgettable tune successfully removes all the excitement of "Boys," opting instead for a Tamla Motown parody and ending up with a song that only really shines with its excellent vocal harmonies—once again, the ace in the early Beatles pack. There's a sudden pause between "I can't conceive of any more . . ." and "Misery!", a direct nod to the arranger's skill, but otherwise this mundane cut doesn't get any pulses racing. On a musicological level, perhaps we could point to the surprisingly funky guitar and bass interplay, and the counterpointed backing vocals, but when did musicological analysis ever get toes tapping, eh?

TOP The Beatles performing at a record store to promote the release of *Please Please Me* in March 1963.

ABOVE The famous "jumping Beatles" photo used on the cover of the "Twist and Shout" EP.

The band receive their silver disc with George Martin in April 1963, for selling 250,000 copies of "Please Please Me."

7 Please Please Me

This classic song is a useful reminder—especially at this early stage—that The Beatles had a sense of wicked humor under those clean-cut exteriors. "Please Please Me" is a milestone in the band's early career, and for good reason. This is a musically adept song, with Lennon's earworm harmonica line mixed at front and center.

SIDE TWO

1 Love Me Do

Chosen as a single because of its listener-friendly melody line and the easily digestible song length, "Love Me Do" doesn't really represent the sound or the ethos of The Beatles, now or later in their career. Long regarded as an anomaly by experts, "Love Me Do," love it or loathe it, remains a curio. Note that the lead harmonica line, a little thin and weedy, sounds completely different to the spacious, reverbed-out equivalent on "Please Please Me."

2 P.S. I Love You

Taking its cue from the catchy love songs that American artists such as Elvis Presley were recording across the Atlantic, "P.S. I Love You" is decidedly of the "Return to Sender" school of ditty. See also "Please Mr. Postman" for the theme of unrequited love via first-class mail. This song is not what you'd call essential, but at least it helped to embed The Beatles in the crucial, and lucrative, love-ballad market. The song does redeem itself by starting suddenly without the benefit of a superfluous intro, grabbing the listener's attention. We should also give props to the earworm of "You, you, you," which you'll be humming all day after a single spin of this treacly song.

3 Baby It's You

What do you know? Another Shirelles cover, although not as gripping as "Boys" by any means. Still, the emotive vocals, both up front and in the background, help to turn the song into something very close to being authentic—well, as close as four lads from the banks of the Mersey could get. "I'm gonna love you any—old—way," intones Lennon, marking his accents out precisely. As has been pointed out elsewhere, he may not have been the most technical singer ever, but there is no doubting the emotional quality of his vocals.

4 Do You Want to Know a Secret

We did indeed, and how coyly Paul and John sang it to us. By the ready-to-rock early sixties, "Do You Want to Know a Secret" must have sounded a little old on the palate for most tastes, but at the same time, The Beatles knew where their bread was buttered—with lovelorn women of all ages—and delivered the songwriting goods accordingly. Keep an ear open for McCartney's elaborate bass line, mixed low so as not to compete with the dominant vocal melody—a sign of the fireworks to come in the future on this traditionally ignored instrument.

5 A Taste of Honey

"Tasting . . . much sweeter . . . than wine!" intoned The Beatles of the eponymous breakfast product, self-evidently and somewhat mysteriously.

As a metaphor for love, the honey image is one that has been used since ancient times, and today "ancient" is exactly how this song sounds in its structure, its production, and its slightly sickly sentiments. That being said, the song departs from the norm in several ways, with a darker, less-optimistic atmosphere than the usual love-song fodder, in its alternation between standard and waltz time—and in its chorus harmony, which is arranged according to folk traditions.

6 There's a Place

As this mixed album comes to a close, on "There's a Place," The Beatles rediscover

"I WANTED TO GET THE BEATLES' FIRST ALBUM RECORDED IN A DAY AND RELEASED VERY QUICKLY."

GEORGE MARTIN

their sense of drive and urgency. Together with the song that followed it, this was the sound of the emerging youthquake on both sides of the Atlantic—and it's the one Beatles track that comes closest to replicating their early sixties live sound on record. You can almost hear the jellybeans being crushed under their Cuban heels, while McCartney hits a falsetto harmony vocal that showcases the man's excellent range. Once more we're treated to a harmonica hook, but what else could they do? No one had invented the electric sitar or the Moog yet.

7 Twist and Shout

Perhaps the ultimate early Beatles song, "Twist and Shout"—covered with varying degrees of success by a plethora of recording artists ever since—still sounds powerfully energetic to this day. Lennon sung his young throat out on this paean to youthful energy, almost literally so (he was suffering from a cold at the time, and a second take had to be abandoned). You can hear the shredded-larynx approach in his performance, inspired by Little Richard and the other rock 'n' roll shouters of the day. The bigger picture is that "Twist and Shout" is essentially a celebration of teenagehood before the concept had begun to be taken seriously by anyone over 20. Songs like this were responsible for kicking the doors of conservatism open—and letting in the light of young, rebellious culture.

Here come The Beatles! On the front page of the *Yorkshire Evening News.*

WITH THE BEATLES

Released **November 22, 1963**

The world stood "with" The Beatles as they prepared to take over—but would album two reveal greater depths than their debut?

. . . .

SIDE ONE

1 It Won't Be Long

Kicking off *With The Beatles* with gusto and aplomb, "It Won't Be Long" is by turns insistent and catchy, mainly thanks to that "Yeah!"-laden chorus. To grasp how essential it was to begin album number two with an upbeat track, we need to consider The Beatles' cultural dominance in late 1963. By now, the quartet were the hottest band in Britain, with teenagers responding in their tens of thousands to songs as optimistic as this one. America, too, literally needed a band like this: bereft of their president in late '63, the public in that country reacted with fervor when The Beatles invaded their TV airwaves early the following year.

2 All I've Got to Do

Indebted as it is to the sound of Smokey Robinson & The Miracles, this track reveals just how much of The Beatles' second-album songwriting was influenced by the structures and arrangements of the great African-American soul music of the day. The track really hits gold with its title line, a four-note descending melody plus jump upwards, that sticks immovably in the listener's ear. It's still cheerful and optimistic, like so much of the early catalogue, with little of the emotional depth that came into the songwriting in 1964 and beyond—but in this context, that's hardly a bad thing.

3 All My Loving

Now, here's a bona fide compositional masterpiece. Adhering to the usual, rather winsome love-song formula, but with a degree of sonic panache which had been lacking on previous ballads, "All My Loving" manages to sound upbeat and plaintive at the same time. The stop-start moments in each verse are the sound of songwriters successfully finding their feet as arrangers, and there's no doubting the efficacy of a descending chord sequence—always the bedrock of the ballad-writer's craft.

4 Don't Bother Me

George Harrison steps in to provide a much-needed touch of retrospection in "Don't Bother Me," the tale of someone in the midst of a relationship breakup. Perhaps the singer's errant girlfriend will return to the fold, but perhaps she won't either: whatever may transpire, he doesn't want to see you. Who hasn't felt this way from time to time? Note also Harrison's excellent guitar solo, an extravagant exercise by the standards of '63, when future shredders such as Eddie Van Halen were just a twinkle in a guitar store owner's eye.

5 Little Child

Swathes of harmonica dominate this nostalgic song, and there's a rumbling piano pushing the track along too, for a welcome change. Lyrically, "Little Child" is a simple dance tune, with Lennon—and McCartney, dropping in some excellent harmonies—requesting the dancefloor pleasure of some teen or other. "Baby take a chance with me," intone our men in this slightest of slight songs, which fades after just one minute and 45 seconds. You almost want to ask yourself why they bothered to include it.

6 Till There Was You

The Beatles give their regards to Broadway on this technically ➥

LEFT The lads amuse themselves with a miniature car racetrack before a show at the Coventry Theatre in November 1963.

ABOVE The band poses together during rehearsals for the ABC Television music show *Thank Your Lucky Stars* in Aston, Birmingham, on October 20, 1963.

competent cover version of Meredith Wilson's theater hit. The jazz chords in the verse reveal the skills of the young guitarists, while McCartney delivers a fantastic vocal performance, hitting wide-interval leaps between notes despite his lack of formal vocal training. Songs such as this one, which point directly at the skills of The Beatles as pure musicians, make a strange juxtaposition against the more meat-and-potatoes dance songs and love ballads elsewhere in their early canon. Then again, an album full of expertly delivered jazz workouts like this track would never have gained them many fans.

7 Please Mr. Postman

Now, here was a genuine oddity. Even at this stage in their careers, The Beatles had shown us that there was more to them than simple rock 'n' roll—and, exciting as

this music had been seven or eight years before 1963, it was definitely time to move on. Perhaps it's best viewed as one of the last signs of clinging onto the safety of traditional, Cavern and Star-Club music that The Beatles displayed before they and their handlers chose to strike out for the choppy—but ultimately more rewarding—waters of originality.

SIDE TWO

1 Roll Over Beethoven

Remember, this album was recorded in the middle of a "beat boom," as the media of the day expressed it—and if you wanted to make money out of music, you were more or less obliged to cover this song

as well as "Long Tall Sally" and "Johnny B. Goode." Real bands played songs like this one, and on this evidence, The Beatles were a real band all right. Lennon and McCartney deliver a unison vocal—no messing about with harmonies here—and a handclap helps a rather hesitant Ringo Starr push the song along. While The Beatles do a reasonable job here, throwing in a polite "Whoo!" here and there, they're not exactly redefining the rock canon with this cover. Hats off for McCartney for a fast-moving bass part, though.

2 Hold Me Tight

"Hold Me Tight" was not held in great esteem by The Beatles in their later years, or indeed by the critics of the period. It's difficult to disagree, although this inoffensive ditty has some redeeming

> ## "WE WENT ON FROM 'LOVE ME DO' TO WRITING DEEPER, MUCH MORE INTENSE THINGS."
>
> **PAUL McCARTNEY**

features, including McCartney's sweet vocal and a relatively thunderous backing track. Starr can be heard fairly clearly for a change, and the call-and-response between the lead and backing vocals is certainly competent. Come on, even rock gods need a filler track now and again—and this was one of those times, all right.

3 You Really Got a Hold on Me

Honed over the passage of time—well before the emergence of their classic self-penned material—this Smokey Robinson & The Miracles cover was a wise addition to The Beatles' recorded repertoire. The time they'd put into it is audible, with a certain finesse in the interpretation, and excellent vocals from Lennon. The guitars nip in and out of tom fills from Starr, each of the musicians evidently aware of the nuances of the arrangement, and well able to take advantage.

4 I Wanna Be Your Man

With an uptempo, near-funky sound that works perfectly to this day, "I Wanna Be Your Man" paints a picture of The Beatles as urgent, lusty young men who had something to say. It's a remarkable song for its era, mostly because it's so relentless: the arrangement powers forward, with the two singers yelling ad hoc interjections. It's classic R&B from the drawer marked "1963," and as such there's no wonder that The Rolling Stones covered it before its writers, Lennon and McCartney, had a chance to record it themselves. The Jagger-and-Richards version is tauter and more urgent, while The Beatles gave it a rough edge that served the song equally well.

5 Devil in Her Heart

George Harrison took lead vocals on this cover (the original version being by American girl group The Donays) and

it's moderately entertaining, if not exactly indispensable. There was a reason why girl-group songs served The Beatles so well—it was all to do with the blokes' expert grasp of falsetto harmonies—and when you think about it, who wouldn't enjoy a combination of rock 'n' roll guitars and luscious vocal layers?

6 Not a Second Time

Neither a love song nor a regretful heartbreaker but somewhere in the middle, the slightly vengeful "Not a Second Time" sees our man warning a deceitful lover off after a regrettable episode of some kind. Droning, a little negative in tone, and heavy on the guitar chords, this song offers a look into the mindset of The Beatles at this pivotal period of transition. Much deeper, more pensive songs were on the way, and the cheesy dance tunes were on the way out: "Not a Second Time" lies somewhere on the dividing line.

7 Money (That's What I Want)

Certain music consumers of the early sixties might have goggled at the egotism of "Money," with its capitalist message, but many others loved it—and to this day the song has a powerful edge that the years have not diminished. Originally a Motown hit for Barrett Strong, the Fab Four's version is a slightly unnerving, fully energized ending to *With The Beatles*—which is itself a step forward from *Please Please Me*, even if the slick love songs and rock 'n' roll parodies haven't fully receded yet. The quartet's grasp of the classic pop-song format was evidently increasing, even if their ability to actually warp the boundaries of popular culture as we know it was still a year or two away.

As the band performed, captions on their close-ups gave each Beatle's name. Lennon's caption also famously said "Sorry girls, he's married."

THE SHOW THAT BROKE AMERICA

Reeling from the assassination of President John F. Kennedy in late 1963, the American public was looking for something new and optimistic—and they were given exactly that when The Beatles made three appearances on *The Ed Sullivan Show* as '64 rolled in.

On February 9, 73 million viewers watched them play "All My Loving," "Till There Was You," "She Loves You," "I Saw Her Standing There," and "I Want to Hold Your Hand." The following week, they added "This Boy" and "From Me to You" in a show broadcast from Miami, and on February 23 a pre-recorded tape of them playing "Twist and Shout," "Please Please Me," and "I Want to Hold Your Hand" went out. A much later show in August 1965, by which point The Beatles were megastars,

paid homage to those earlier, apocalyptic appearances. Those three dates have been celebrated and re-celebrated many times over the decades, and it's easy to see why. If you ask more or less any successful American rock musician born between 1945 and 1955 what their primary influences are, "The Beatles on *Ed Sullivan*" will invariably be among their answers.

A HARD DAY'S NIGHT

Released July 10, 1964

Ker-chinggg! What was that mysterious chord? We may never know—but we do know that *A Hard Day's Night* was the first genuinely classic Beatles album.

SIDE ONE

1 A Hard Day's Night

Opening with that unknowable guitar chord, "A Hard Day's Night" adds the throwaway quote by Ringo of the title to a bracing structure: accelerates hard and never looks back. The listener is gripped from the start by the demonstration of Lennon and McCartney's low-register singing skills, all the way through to the surprisingly tender guitar arpeggios that end the song. It's another near-perfect single in a run of near-perfect singles, and one of the finest opening songs on any LP ever. What's funny, when you think about it, is that "A Hard Day's Night" is essential listening for anyone into sixties rock—even though revolutionary sixties rock, as we think of it now, was still a year or so away as The Beatles rolled into 1964.

2 I Should Have Known Better

Now here's a catchy song—from the insistent harmonica, via the vocal melody, to the unexpected chord change in the verses. Strummed chords at certain places courtesy of George Harrison's Rickenbacker add depth, as does a noticeable improvement in production, now that we're a couple of years into The Beatles' career. You can also hear how Lennon and Harrison have refined their lead guitar skills, having wisely learned that a simple melody outshines a flurry of notes any day of the week. Sure, The Beatles are still a step-change or two away from throwing in unusual changes or arrangements, so this song ends with the expected coda and fade—but just you wait: more innovative songwriting was effectively just around the corner.

3 If I Fell

In lesser hands, "If I Fell" could have been a cloying ballad, but with The Beatles this song achieves a better outcome than the sum of its parts. Listen out for that "Help me!" from Lennon in the intro, immediately reminiscent of the "Al-feee!" from the 1966 movie *Alfie*—later a hit for Cilla Black, and almost as reminiscent of Swinging London as the Fab Four themselves. The vocal harmonies in this song are so seamless as to be sublime, the previous couple of years of studying studio techniques having paid off for Lennon and McCartney. The result is something of a heartbreaker ("I couldn't stand the pain") and also one of the sweetest ballads in the entire Beatles canon.

4 I'm Happy Just to Dance with You

Simple sentiments abound on "I'm Happy Just to Dance with You," which could well have been an older, *Please Please Me*-era Beatles song had its production not been so much clearer and fuller than anything from that album. McCartney's bass parts now have roundness as well as thud; you can hear Starr's hi-hat clearly for the first time; and the layers of different guitars are actually discernible. What's amusing, given all that, is that this song is so sixth-form in its lyrics. It is literally about a) wanting to dance with someone, and b) being disappointed if said dance does not occur. Not that lyrical depth is essential in order to enjoy a song—it's just that so much thematic innovation was poised to come from the songwriting of this unique band that it's funny to analyze the very last of their simple love songs.

The album's titular phrase was a malapropism once uttered by Ringo. The band jokingly referred to these as "Ringo-isms."

> **"THE STRIDENT GUITAR CHORD WAS THE PERFECT LAUNCH."**
>
> **GEORGE MARTIN**

5 And I Love Her

On the subject of innovation, here's tenderness personified. "And I Love Her" is an exquisitely refined song, with its tempo, melody, and structure as finely gauged and fragile as any other song from any other era. It comes across so much more that way because it has been written by a band who had formerly specialized in the most raucous, unreconstructed rock 'n' roll. Can you imagine the jaws dropping among The Beatles' fanbase when they first heard this crystalline song? It remains a thing of beauty to this day.

6 Tell Me Why

If you had to accuse any of The Beatles' songs of being filler, then "Tell Me Why" would not be one of them, even though hardly anyone has heard of it. Our senses thrum to the sound of The Beatles' musical dexterity here, with a swing feel and excellent close vocal harmonies—maybe only matched by the Everly Brothers in the pre-Crosby, Stills & Nash era. The writing was on the wall for the pre-Beatles generation of entertainers, because bands like this one could deliver heartfelt lyrics as well as any of the old guard—but accompanied by a rocking soundtrack that was completely new.

7 Can't Buy Me Love

The presence of "Can't Buy Me Love" on *A Hard Day's Night* makes it more of a heavyweight album than would otherwise have been the case. It's even better when heard as the backing to the accompanying film's classic "breakout" set piece of goonery, because the song comes with a mesmerizing sense of energy and rebellion. Is it a complaint, a protest, a statement of intent? Perhaps all of those things, embedded in an arrangement that simply oozes adrenaline. One of the most upbeat songs that The Beatles ever wrote, "Can't Buy Me Love" sounds like the work of three bands kicking butt as one, not simply a single foursome. ➦

The band poses in the cockpit as they are about to fly to Liverpool for the northern premiere of *A Hard Day's Night*.

Beatlemania was in full swing—thousands of fans gathered to see the band arrive for the Liverpool premiere of *A Hard Day's Night* in July 1964.

SIDE TWO

1 Any Time at All

Something of a harbinger of The Beatles' future direction, "Any Time at All" generates real momentum as it powers along. Much of its musical propulsion comes from Starr's enthusiastic tub-thumping, although here—as with elsewhere in the catalogue—he chooses to play with economy rather than panache. Hear how Lennon and McCartney trade yells of the title phrase, with Lennon taking a lower, more abrasive register while McCartney delivers an expert yelp at the top of his range. The song slides to a halt with a single chord, a trick that was rapidly becoming one of The Beatles' signature songwriting moves.

2 I'll Cry Instead

Great as *A Hard Day's Night* undoubtedly is, it isn't all gold. Here and there, as with "I'll Cry Instead," The Beatles retread familiar ground—that of the spurned lover. Lyrically, it's a touch unusual by modern standards: Lennon sings of wanting to break so many hearts that the girls had better be hidden away from him, at least until his own broken heart is mended. Until then, he warns forlornly, he'll cry instead, making this something of an empty threat. The result is that when this song is held up against The Beatles' best works, "I'll Cry Instead" can only be ranked as a minor footnote, and a slightly strange one at that.

3 Things We Said Today

The Beatles sounded rather depressed on this downbeat track—although this is not meant as a critique, because it's a clear indicator of the deep, soul-searching songs to come. By that point, however, their early performance trick of singing a unison vocal line would be long gone: indeed, this form of singing marks out any Beatles song that uses it as a relatively early one in the band's career. So what do we have here? Arguably, "Things We Said Today" is something of an unheralded gem that points the way to later material such as "Baby's in Black." It fades, rather sadly and ominously, leaving a question mark in the listener's mind.

4 When I Get Home

The Beatles boogie hard on this rather fine tune, in which Lennon and McCartney sing about how happy they're going to be when they see a girl tonight. "I'm gonna love her till the cows come home," they tell us informatively, with a particularly fine vocal display from McCartney, whose performance in the song's midsection is especially strong. The two singers warble through the repeated nonsense phrase "Whoa-oh-ho, ha!" presumably because they're emoting here about subjects too sensitive to be enunciated in lyrics.

5 You Can't Do That

The all-time great rocker "You Can't Do That" is essentially an aggressive blues song, driven along by Lennon's introspective lyrics, and coupled with Harrison and McCartney's thrilling backing vocals. What's really interesting about this song is that the lyrics are proscriptive, informing someone of the things they're not permitted to do, but they're also vulnerable. "I've got something to say that might cause you pain," begin the lyrics, almost timidly, before Lennon rattles off what is essentially a list of commands. Again, by modern standards, what he's saying is virtually unacceptable. It's down to the listener whether to judge the song by the standards of 1964 or today.

The studio album was released shortly after the film of the same name in the UK. The musical comedy was the band's first foray into film.

6 I'll Be Back

This song is a clear sign of the Fab Four's growing maturity as artists, as well as the increasing diversity of their material. Can we detect an affectionate lean on the descending chords of Del Shannon's "Runaway"? Either way, what a fine way to sign off this album, The Beatles' most advanced to date. In retrospect, *A Hard Day's Night*—with its reliance on self-penned material—raised the bar for pretty much every other pop group of 1964. It's a fine time capsule, if dated in many ways.

LEFT Rehearsing for the Royal Command Performance at the Prince of Wales Theatre, November 1963.

STAR-CLUB, HAMBURG, MAY '62

BELOW The Fab Four, circa 1963. Back then the band had no idea how influential they would become.

ABOVE Brian Epstein encouraged the "clean cut" look so that parents wouldn't mind their kids listening to rock 'n' roll.

THE CAVERN CLUB, LIVERPOOL, AUG '61

ABOVE Filming for an appearance on *Late Scene Extra* in Manchester, November 1963.

ABOVE A publicity photo of the band taken aboard The Salvor in Liverpool, circa September 1962.

RELAXING BACKSTAGE, NOV '62.

BEATLES FOR SALE

Released **December 4, 1964**

Equal halves rock 'n' roll and sophisticated introspection, this album left The Beatles' fanbase a touch confused.

·····································

George and John on *Shindig!* in October 1964. They played "Kansas City/Hey, Hey, Hey, Hey," "I'm a Loser," and "Boys" on the show.

SIDE ONE

1 No Reply

Who started an album with a sad song about unrequited love in the chirpy days of 1964? Only a band with a bunch of hits behind them, the confidence to experiment, and a manager and producer who were sympathetic to the cause, that's who. "No Reply" is full of surprises, from the sudden barks of the chorus—wailed with sincere misery, it seems—to the chunky drums and the sudden end. The song finishes up with the depressing conclusion that there's "No Reply," and that there never will be. It's one of The Beatles' most affecting performances, and what's more, they deliver it in a downbeat, almost bossa nova timbre. You can imagine the surprise of the kid who bought the album and was expecting it to supply cheerful vibes right from the start.

2 I'm a Loser

How much influence did Bob Dylan have over The Beatles? On "I'm a Loser," he casts a long shadow, as this song benefits from strummed acoustic guitar, introspective lyrics, and a rough-edged harmonica. "I'm not what I appear to be," sings John Lennon, a message that would competently represent the whole of this transitional album. Although the expected unison and harmony vocals are still here, as well as the warbling harmonica and simple guitar solos—all of which mark this song, and album, as featuring in the early-career canon—The Beatles were clearly on their way somewhere different with songs such as this one.

The 2016 documentary *The Beatles: Eight Days a Week—The Touring Years* captures what life was like for The Beatles as they toured extensively between 1962 and 1966.

3 Baby's in Black

Something of a folk ballad, "Baby's in Black" comes with an infectious chorus and a sterling exhibition on the drums from Ringo Starr. However, the band is far from upbeat on this song, asking us the repeated question, "What can I do?" Of course, we don't have an answer for them, which prompts us to listen carefully as Lennon and McCartney explain what their problem is. As the song explains, it's a complex scenario, with the object of affection squarely focused on an absent paramour—and dressed in appropriately miserable garb—rather than giving a thought to our lovelorn Liverpudlian lads. Note the amazing falsetto harmony mid song from McCartney.

4 Rock and Roll Music

The Beatles' rendition of Chuck Berry's canonical "Rock and Roll Music" is one of the better performances on this album. It's every bit the equal of the original, although Berry disciples—and even The Beatles themselves—might regard such a claim as heresy. Still, consider the close unison of the guitars, McCartney's twisty bass, and the sheer optimistic energy barked out in the vocals, and you'll understand why this version of the classic tune is so highly regarded. In some ways the song remained something of a mission statement for this most devoted of rock 'n' roll covers acts, in particular for Lennon, who sometimes sported the mandatory quiff and leathers into the seventies.

5 I'll Follow the Sun

This slight McCartney composition was dredged up from the Hamburg days, and presents our man in something of a bitter mood, despite its lovely pastoral backing. In the song he warns an unidentified lover—there's a lot of these in the early- to mid-career Beatles songs—that in due course she will regret not fancying him to the degree that he feels would be justified. It's incongruous by today's standards, of course, placing the bloke and his ego squarely at front and center. The idea that, until she snaps out of it, he'll follow the sun, doesn't make a whole lot of sense, unless that's a metaphor for something or other. Note that the sweet acoustic backing nods directly towards McCartney's future classic of the genre, "Blackbird."

6 Mr. Moonlight

Apart from a fairly annoying Hammond organ solo from McCartney, this song is pleasant enough, with beautifully layered vocal harmonies that sit rather starkly against the meat-and-potatoes backing. Perhaps George Martin and the recording team had recently nailed the art of committing close harmonies to tape, while the band themselves had yet to refine their playing skills accordingly? ➡

> **"RECORDING *BEATLES FOR SALE* DIDN'T TAKE LONG. BASICALLY IT WAS OUR STAGE SHOW, WITH SOME NEW SONGS."**
>
> **PAUL McCARTNEY**

7 Kansas City / Hey, Hey, Hey, Hey

Making the most of the Little Richard original, this cover version has many highlights. Listen out for McCartney's excellent lead vocal, ably supported by a slightly nasal harmony from Lennon in the background, and the honky-tonk piano part. As with "Rock and Roll Music," The Beatles scored highly on this take on an overseas classic by giving their full commitment to the sound and ethos of rock 'n' roll. Yes, the song was written by an African-American eccentric amid a morass of conflicting race and gender politics, while The Beatles were (by that point, very wealthy) white boys from an English seaport. However, both original and cover version belt out the music and lyrics with tons of energy, underpinned by the maxim that there's no need to sing a word when you can just as easily scream it.

SIDE TWO

1 Eight Days a Week

This song is one of the very first in The Beatles' recorded catalogue thus far to hint that there might be more diverse music ahead than mere rock 'n' roll covers and love songs. That descending chord sequence in the intro—with no warning and no opening setup—is essentially a sped-up "Lucy in the Sky with Diamonds" without the trippy bits. The title, too, may well have the wacky, throwaway feel of "A Hard Day's Night," but equally it's a play on words that would endure deep into the *Sgt. Pepper* era, just three years later. The telltale sign of a song from this early in The Beatles' career is, of course, the presence of an "Ooh"—in this case, the very first word—as well as a certain cheerful optimism in the lyrics. Here, Lennon and McCartney sing about how good it feels to be in love with a girl: there are none of the unsettling fripperies that would adorn this sentiment once the years passed and the acid kicked in.

2 Words of Love

This faithful imitation of the Buddy Holly classic has its moments, in particular the double-tracked harmonies from George

JOHN plays tambourine during a recording session for *Beatles for Sale* in October 1964, with producer George Martin (left).

"WE WERE BECOMING MORE RELAXED WITH OURSELVES, AND MORE COMFORTABLE IN THE STUDIO."

GEORGE HARRISON

POSING for a promotional shot for *Another Beatles Christmas Show*. The popular run of shows featured a mix of music, pantomime, and comedy, with guest stars.

5 I Don't Want to Spoil the Party

There's much to love in this song, in which a sequence of catchy chord changes accompany the complaints of the devoted duo about, yes, a lover who is spurning their advances. Informatively, they set the scene of a gathering from which, having had a few drinks and concluding that it's no fun, they depart. Still, they promise always to love whoever it is despite whatever it is she's done. Bighearted of them, you'll agree.

6 What You're Doing

The pensive "What You're Doing" was written by McCartney, supposedly about his doomed love affair with Jane Asher, and as such departs slightly from the norm. Mind you, what "the norm" actually is on this record of two halves is up for debate. Heartfelt love songs like this one, whether happy or sad, don't sit particularly comfortably alongside raucous rock 'n' roll covers, after all.

7 Everybody's Trying to Be My Baby

Another more or less satisfying facsimile of a well-known song, "Everybody's Trying to Be My Baby" is an identikit copy of the Carl Perkins original. This is, perhaps, understandable in the light of The Beatles' gradual move away from covers to original compositions. Maybe *Beatles for Sale* as a whole is best appreciated as an album that falls prey to The Beatles' incredibly hectic schedule, which meant that a slew of cover versions were needed to fill the gaps between original songs of the quality of "Eight Days a Week," "Baby's in Black," and "I'm a Loser." Time is money, after all.

Harrison, but where does it fit on this curious collection of songs? The playing is as thin as can be, with the mix focused almost solely on the chiming guitars—which is understandable, as it's a song written by an influential guitarist—but the lack of anything more than a cursory bass and drum accompaniment makes the track a tad lightweight. Fading out after two minutes, the song shouts "filler" in comparison to the more heavyweight big hitters here, but let's be charitable—a lot of Beatles fans prefer this era of their recording career for its innocence and simplicity.

3 Honey Don't

This song, taken from the flipside of Carl Perkins' amazing "Blue Suede Shoes" single, both benefits and suffers from Ringo's vocal limitations. Sure, his emoting adds a pleasantly naïve air to the song, but at the same time, he makes it a little difficult to take seriously. What does work, however, is the competent rock 'n' roll backing, with an excellent walking bass line from McCartney and an exquisitely gauged rockabilly guitar solo. When it came to classic R&R sounds, this band knew exactly what they were doing.

4 Every Little Thing

Who else could afford to relegate a tune of this quality to the status of an album filler? Chiming guitars and sweet vocal harmonies introduce the affecting "Every Little Thing," on which our chaps celebrate the generous spirit of yet another woman. ("I will love her forever, for I know our love will never die.") It's the polar opposite of all those miserable songs that predict future regrets for any potential lover who doesn't seem eager.

THE FAMILIAR SIGHT OF FAINTING FANS

FANS SAY FAREWELL AT THE AIRPORT, FEB '65

TARA BOYS

ABOVE The hysteria of the Beatlemania phenomenon spread from the UK to the US and beyond.

HELP! BEATLES HELP!

BEATLES HELP!

BAND-AID plastic strip

Make A Date With THE BEATLES

DEC 22

Get Your BEATLES! BUTTONS HERE!

THE BEATLES

THE BEATLES

I LOVE the BEATLES

I·B·F·C·
NO.
John Lennon
Ringo Starr

BEATLES' H

SUPPLY IS LIMITED
For that special Beatlemaniac.

Yes BEATLE FANS
Yesterday our troubles seemed so far away. So come together now and discover what millions have before, that LOVE is all you need! Experience what magic their mop-tops brought to others. Take this card, hold tight and SHAKE!

ACTUALLY contains a lock of hair from one of the Fab Four.

THE HEART OF THE

PAUL POSES WITH A FANZINE, '64

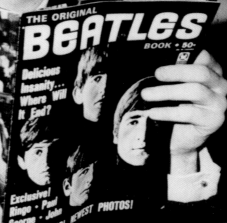

ABOVE Officers struggle to hold back fans outside Buckingham Palace as the band receive their MBEs, October 1965.

BELOW An estimated 300,000 fans lined the streets for the band's arrival in Adelaide, Australia in June 1964.

LEFT A selection of Beatles memorabilia, including locks of hair "for that special Beatlemaniac!"

AN AUSSIE WELCOME, JUNE '64

Images Hulton-Deutsch Collection/Corbis via Getty Images (Police); Pictorial Press Ltd/Alamy (Painting); Trinity Mirror/Mirrorpix/Alamy (plane); Central Press/Getty Images (taxi); Blank Archives/Getty Images (merch); Keystone/Getty Images (adelaide '64); GAB Archive/Redferns/Getty Images (crowd); Michael Ochs Archives/Getty Images (McCartney)

HELP!

Released August 6, 1965

With *Help!*, The Beatles enter
their mature songwriting
phase—and the results speak
for themselves. At least, most
of the time.

· · · · · · · · · · · · · · ·

SIDE ONE

1 Help!

For many music fans in the mid-sixties,
"Help!" was simply a piece of good-time
Beatles pop, although there was no doubting
the sincerity of the impassioned vocals and
the descending, Chet Atkins-style guitar lines.
However, if you pay close attention to the lyrics,
underneath the commercial sheen, they seem
to be loaded with despair—John Lennon's
self-described mid-career misery in evidence.
Stick with this wonderful song, though, because
everything about it reveals the sophistication
that The Beatles had now achieved as
songwriters. There's the straight-out-of-the-
blocks start; the supremely clever vocal stacks
in the chorus; the aforementioned three-note
guitar licks; and that final, epic chord, something
of a questioning, jazz-indebted construction.
These boys were getting good.

2 The Night Before

Another stone-cold classic follows the title
cut, with the expert chorus of "The Night
Before" generating an atmosphere of giddy
euphoria—or rather, continuing it where "Help!"
left off. The electric piano and guitar solo give
the song an extra push, with the ace in the song's
pack being the "aye-aye-aye" melody in the verse
lines. Repeated every few seconds, this earworm
burrows its way deep into the listener's cerebral
cortex and will not be shifted, as its creators
knew very well. Songs like this make it easy to
understand why Lennon and McCartney would
say to each other, "Let's write a swimming pool,"
before sitting down to compose, knowing full
well how much cash would flow their way if they
came up with a hookline as efficient as this one.

3 You've Got to Hide Your Love Away

"You've Got to Hide Your Love Away" is a heady confection of folk-rock Americana. Note the nicely judged flute solo on the instrumental break, a first for The Beatles, but absolutely not the last time they would break with their own tradition and incorporate non-rock 'n' roll instrumentation into their songwriting. Now, much has been written over the years about Bob Dylan's influence on this song, and obviously there's a reasonable argument to be made that Lennon was indeed heavily influenced by Professor Zimmerman here. Still, the song's strength is all in its subtle vocal, not an asset usually associated with Dylan, and something of a revelation for Lennon fans accustomed to his earlier rockabilly roar. Consider that when you listen to this song: it is a point well made that the late Lennon may not have been a technically gifted singer, but he sure was an emotional one.

4 I Need You

The love lives of the various Beatles would prove to be a rich seam of inspiration for the group, be it Jane Asher, Linda Eastman, Cynthia Powell, Yoko Ono, or, on this occasion, Pattie Boyd—who was George Harrison's muse when he wrote this downcast tale of unwanted time spent apart from a loved one. Musically, it's sprightly enough, with stabs of chiming guitar rather than the usual strummed chords making it a more refined listen than the usual balladry. There's plenty of percussion, too, which adds a lively edge to all the emoting.

5 Another Girl

Rather like "She's a Woman," this McCartney composition defeats all opposition through its backbeat and its country and western counterpoint. Questioning guitar licks populate the verse, while the chords move around and the vocals counterpoint the arrangement very skilfully. It's a song that demands your attention because there's so much going on, but at the same time you're happy to give it the attention that it requires. Note the end flurry of Eric Clapton-style lead guitar. ➺

ABOVE The band poses for photographs as they are presented with Gold Records—awarded for *Help!* reaching one million dollars of US sales—by Capitol Records president Alan Livingston (right).

TOP Ringo, Paul, John, and George in their disguises while filming a scene in *Help!*. The title of the film was decided first, and the theme song was written by Lennon to match.

Words: Joel McIver. Images: The Beatles (album cover); Michael Ochs Archives/Getty Images (gold records); c) Everett Collection Inc/Alamy (disguises)

ABOVE The band relaxing during a rehearsal for *Thank Your Lucky Stars* in March 1965. They performed "Eight Days a Week," "Yes It Is," and "Ticket to Ride" on the show.

BELOW RIGHT McCartney performing a solo rendition of "Yesterday" on *Blackpool Night Out* in August 1965. It was the first time the song was performed on British television.

6 You're Going to Lose That Girl

This is one of the better tracks on the *Help!* album, and one that stands up well today, even in the glare of 21st-century sunlight. Who doesn't respond to a ravishing falsetto in the middle of a melody line? The Beatles were all too aware of this funky little songwriting trick, and what's more, they knew how to write a theme that would make people listen. What exactly had the object of The Beatles' advice done to risk losing his girlfriend, and what exactly qualified the Fab Four to advise the chap on the subject? Only they knew.

7 Ticket to Ride

Instantly recognizable from its opening guitar chimes, "Ticket to Ride" is nothing less than a dazzling step forward in The Beatles' songwriting, and points the way directly towards the full-blown psychedelia of songs such as "Rain." Here,

the singers sound absolutely heartsick, with the sadness of rejection embodied in their lost lover's ticket out of their lives. It was the first song recorded for *Help!*, and marked a change in the band's recording processes, as they recorded the drums and bass before overdubbing with the remaining instruments and vocals. "Ticket to Ride" was also the first Beatles track to feature McCartney on lead guitar.

———

SIDE TWO

1 Act Naturally

"Act Naturally" shows The Beatles' adroitness at injecting humor in order to perk up otherwise standard material, as evidenced by their lively take of this country and western hit for Buck Owens. It's probably best not to attempt any serious analysis

with this little curio, other than to note that for musicians of a certain age, the "singing cowboy" trope imported from American TV in the fifties was hugely influential—just as *Star Wars* was for anyone born two decades later than The Beatles were, to put it in a modern context.

2 It's Only Love

Listen carefully to John Lennon's vocals on "It's Only Love" and it's almost as if he can barely conceal his embarrassment at having to sing this song. Unfortunately, it conjures up something of a sickly sweet aftertaste, and remains completely at odds with The Beatles in their songwriting pomp. Whatever is going on with the guitars in the background of this mercifully short song doesn't sound great, either. Masters of songcraft though The Beatles assuredly were at this point, they occasionally failed to hit the bullseye, or—as in the case of this song—they missed the target completely.

"WHEN 'HELP!' CAME OUT, I WAS ACTUALLY CRYING OUT FOR HELP. MOST PEOPLE THINK IT'S JUST A FAST ROCK 'N' ROLL SONG."

JOHN LENNON

3 You Like Me Too Much

Another misfire, unfortunately. Like an overexcited teenager, this is all arms and legs and has none of the sublime qualities we would later come to expect from the quiet Beatle, George Harrison. Yes, the cowboy-saloon piano of the intro has a certain cinematic charm, and of course the close vocal harmonies are satisfying, but there's only so many cloying songs about failed or otherwise love affairs that the human ear can stand.

4 Tell Me What You See

Fortunately, "Tell Me What You See" works perfectly well, largely because it's in direct contrast to the lightweight material that we've been subjected to a moment ago. Perhaps this Latin-infused number is a little lacking in emotive substance ("Look into these eyes now / Tell me what you see"), but it swings nicely and will cause the listener to tap a foot in occasional appreciation. The rounded mix and counterpointed guitar accents make the song sound rather more advanced than its lyrics and title would imply.

5 I've Just Seen a Face

Now, songwriting landmarks such as "Yesterday" would go on to rank far higher in McCartney's songwriting career than "I've Just Seen a Face"—but let's give the song the space it deserves. Here, McCartney intones a rapid-fire vocal against a background that is pure Americana—more Lubbock, Texas than Liverpool, Merseyside. If you're in the mood for some doe-eyed romanticism, look no further.

6 Yesterday

The big unanswered question here is, "Does Paul sing 'Yesterday came suddenly,' or 'Yes, today came suddenly?'" The first received wisdom; the second is a better, if usually rejected, alternative. Whatever the answer, this level of microanalysis shows you how huge an impact "Yesterday" made on the world of music. A ballad to end all ballads, the song is improved immeasurably by the George Martin-managed strings ensemble and McCartney's choice of a lower vocal range than usual. McCartney himself later wrote in his memoirs that he had no idea where the song's immortal vocal melodies came from, and that he has rigorously checked his inspirations over the years to see where they might have come from. They fell directly into his brain from some beneficent deity, apparently.

7 Dizzy Miss Lizzy

This cover version of the Larry Williams original was fitted in around a hectic recording schedule for The Beatles' second cinematic feature. After the dazzling pop moments that preceded it, "Dizzy Miss Lizzy" sounds a touch uninspired, perhaps as something of an afterthought. The film of *Help!* itself is a rather thin premise, and some of the tracks included on this album are little better—but look, the big hits were hits for a reason, and The Beatles were now on an upward trajectory that showed little sign of slowing down.

"THE volume of screams drowned everything else out," recalled Ringo in *The Beatles Anthology.*

TRIUMPH AT SHEA STADIUM

On August 15, 1965, The Beatles rolled up to Shea Stadium, a baseball venue in New York. It was the first date of that year's summer tour of North America, and Beatlemania had progressed from beyond a mere fad to an absolutely primal cultural force. A record was set that day for the size of the audience—estimated to be 55,600 fans—most of whom made their presence felt with screams of appreciation that caused venue staff to cover their ears in alarm.

In playing this seminal show, The Beatles kick-started two important phenomena. Firstly, the concept of rock bands being commercially able to sell out massive venues; in this sense The Beatles were followed by Led Zeppelin in the seventies and Duran Duran in the eighties. Secondly, and equally importantly, a whole new area of performance audio technology was forced to evolve. On that day at Shea Stadium, The Beatles couldn't hear themselves because of the woefully inadequate public-address system, which couldn't hope to outdo the insane noise levels emanating from the crowd. No one in the audience could hear them, either—leading directly to the rise of massive PA systems in subsequent years.

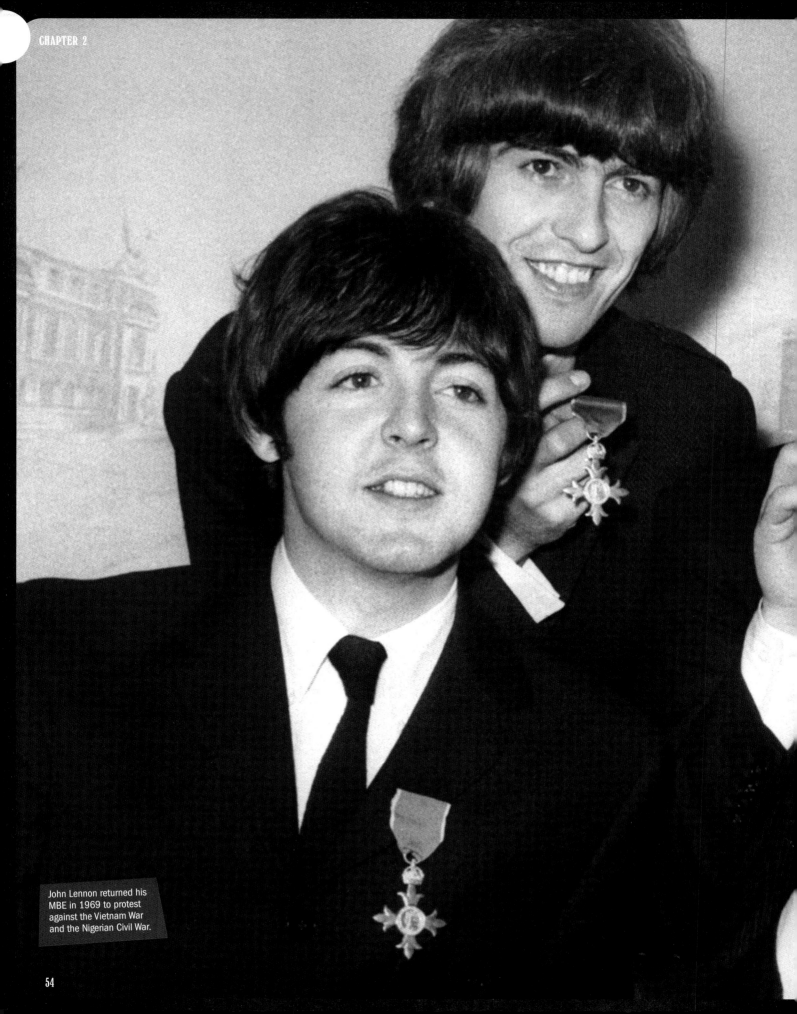

John Lennon returned his MBE in 1969 to protest against the Vietnam War and the Nigerian Civil War.

HONORED BY THE QUEEN

You know your band has made it big, even today, if the royal family sees fit to pin an MBE to your chest—but in October 1965, when pop music was less popular at Buckingham Palace than corgi urine, The Beatles getting MBEs was nothing less than revolutionary. It emerged that quite a few former honors recipients actually returned their own medals in protest at Queen Elizabeth II deigning to welcome these Liverpudlian rascals into the circles of the elite.

So why did the Palace agree to award the honors? Presumably in an attempt to keep the media at bay—a campaign for the MBEs to be awarded had been promoted by *Melody Maker* magazine—but also because The Beatles' overseas sales were bringing staggering amounts of money into the UK. Not that the band themselves particularly gave a hoot: the famous story goes that the four cheeky chaps smoked a joint in the Palace bathrooms before stepping out to meet Her Majesty. Some doubt has been cast on this anecdote—the offending item may have simply been a humble cigarette—but it's a great story anyway.

RUBBER SOUL

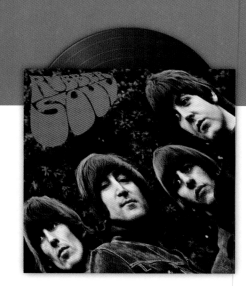

Released **December 3, 1965**

The immortal *Rubber Soul* sees The Beatles stretch their songwriting wings and fly, with not a rock 'n' roll cover version in sight.

· · · · · · · · · · · · · · · · · · · ·

SIDE ONE

1 Drive My Car

What a risky way to start an album—but that risk pays off admirably. "Drive My Car," which would have been a novelty song in the hands of any other band, steers the right course throughout, even though it's quirky, eccentric, and even a little bit annoying. Still, the humor in the lyrics and in the rollicking backing music stands the test of time more than adequately—it even competes with "Back in the U.S.S.R." for the crown of Best Beatles Album Opener, if you ask more than a few of its devotees. Was the act of driving a car a metaphor for something else? With songwriters as potent as John Lennon and Paul McCartney, it was probably better not to ask . . . so let's just enjoy the ride.

2 Norwegian Wood (This Bird Has Flown)

Just as The Beatles' songwriting rivals—in late '65, The Beach Boys, The Who, and possibly the up-and-coming Kinks and Yardbirds—were beginning to advance their skills, build their profile, and snap at their Cuban heels, our boys stepped up their game dramatically. A notable expansion to The Beatles' oeuvre in more ways than one, "Norwegian Wood" was where their lyrics, thanks at least in part to the influence of their new friend Bob Dylan, became more opaque, and at the same time more open to interpretation. The girl in the song—a working woman, as you'll recall—offers the narrator some wine; they talk until three; he famously "crawls off to sleep in the bath." There's a lot of unspoken subtext there, and Beatles fans' feverish imaginations worked hard to speculate

what that subtext might be. Cleverly, Lennon and McCartney left it to us to figure out, focusing instead on innovations such as the sitar that delivers the main melody line.

3 You Won't See Me

What is it about this song that reminds the listener so much of the theme to the old TV show, *Minder*? Perhaps it's the guitar stabs and the busy bass, plus that geezer-ish vocal performance. None of this makes the song unlikeable, but perhaps these elements detract somewhat for anyone who was expecting journeys into the caverns of the psyche, "Norwegian Wood"-style. In any case, the subject matter of "You Won't See Me" has a certain fascination for McCartney watchers. It

tackles McCartney's growing disenchantment in his relationship at the time with Jane Asher, who must have been delighted to discover that fact when it was first revealed to her. That's the downside of going out with a rock star, presumably.

4 Nowhere Man

Where do we start with this pivotal song, not just for The Beatles' career but for virtually all confessional, stream-of-consciousness lyric songwriting that followed? Rarely has such thematic nihilism been accompanied by such wondrous music, a wash of warm vocal, and musicianly background that lends Lennon's words a soft, pensive backdrop. As for what the great man is ➤➤

LEFT Workers in the production line at the EMI Factory in Hayes, Middlesex, UK, manufacturing the *Rubber Soul* LP in November 1965.

ABOVE John, Ringo, Paul, and George pose for a portrait while working in the studio, circa 1965.

ABOVE Paul and John backstage at the Glasgow Odeon, where they began their final UK tour, for a press conference on the day of *Rubber Soul*'s release.

MAIN The Fab Four greet fans as they return to the UK from their US tour, September 1965.

Images: Evening Standard/Hulton Archive/Getty Images (main); Daily Record/Mirrorpix/Mirrorpix/Getty Images (inset)

"THE DIRECTION WAS MOVING AWAY FROM THE POPPY STUFF."

PAUL McCARTNEY

actually telling us, it seems that the Nowhere Man is a character with zero attributes ("Doesn't have a point of view, knows not where he's going to"). In fact, this reduction to nothing is the whole point of the character and of the song, forcing us to ask ourselves what we are that the Nowhere Man is not. Perhaps we too are Nowhere People—and perhaps, given the extraordinary thought processes which The Beatles were going through in the mid to late sixties, the band were telling us that this was no bad thing. Why not give everything up and simply *be*?

5 Think for Yourself

This fast-paced track penned by McCartney about "standing on your own two feet" is succinct, both in its brevity and its message. Had McCartney been reading a bit of Aleister Crowley, by any chance? Mid-sixties intellectuals like our friends in The Beatles would have had a field day discussing those "do what thou wilt" ideas in a smoky parlor or two, intermingled with the otherworldly thinking of the gurus whose philosophies matched theirs. This is speculation, of course, but it's completely plausible given the simple music, prioritizing message over accompaniment, and the mind-bending era of evolution in thought that the period of 1965 to 1970 encouraged. It's an era we can't easily comprehend today, so pay attention to these lyrics—they're the voice of reason, calling to us from the past. That is, at least, how Lennon and McCartney would have wished their art to be conveyed, all these years later.

6 The Word

Presaging the coming of the counterculture, the message is love, and the exuberance of The Beatles' performance is infectious, thanks to Starr's resolutely backward drum fills, the eccentric piano playing of McCartney, and the expertly falsetto harmonies on the chorus. "Say the word and be like me," they warble, for all the world like a Scouse Monkees tribute band. The importance of the word "love" was, of course, the core of the entire hippie movement, and as 1965 moved into '66 and then the glorious Summer of Love that was 1967, the message became louder, clearer, and more serious. The Vietnam War was at its peak around this time; anti-Communist fear, McCarthyism, and nuclear-war paranoia were infesting the minds of the public in America, where The Beatles had millions of followers; and along with the expansion of everyone's minds came a creeping fear based on those social ills. Given all that, the message of "The Word" is not only understandable, it's the only thing that made contextual sense.

7 Michelle

Memorable for McCartney's grammar-school French—the height of sophistication at the time, as readers of a certain age will remember—as well as the jokiness of the lyrics ("I want you, I want you, I want you / I think you know by now"), "Michelle" is that rare thing, a unique song. Similar sentiments exist throughout the rest of The Beatles' catalogue, of course, but rarely in so reductive a form, and almost never stepping outside a very English perspective—those early German-language recordings aside, of course. So what is McCartney actually saying here? Well, we know he's worried about a failure to communicate; we also know he feels extremely tender towards our French *petite amie* because the music indicates as much. With its classical guitar accompaniment, chanteur-style vocal delivery, and yes, those awesomely amateurish French phrases, "Michelle" is easily the most "ballady" of any ballad The Beatles ever wrote—and that includes "Yesterday," a lament rather than a love song. ➠

1 What Goes On

Moving on from the psychobabble and the exploration of the mind, this song gallops along at a fair old pace, which—unfortunately—can't detract from a "courageous" vocal from Ringo Starr, undemanding lyrics, and some guitar licks from George that we've definitely heard before. Is that a little harsh? Possibly. One aspect of The Beatles' genius, after all, was that they were able to invoke universal harmony one minute and then sing about kitchen-sink matters the next. In this way, they anchored their more supernatural musings to the ground, rather than going "full Pink Floyd" and leaving for the stratosphere. Perhaps there was too much Liverpool in them for that—too much rock 'n' roll, too much Cavern Club, and too much of the mean streets of Hamburg. Either way, "What Goes On" isn't exactly out of place here, but you'll need to be prepared for something of an abrupt about-face.

2 Girl

"Girl" is a gorgeous song, but a rather unusual one too, at least when you attempt to isolate its influences. The other Beatles' backing of John Lennon's sighing, somewhat world-weary vocals is a little redolent of a German two-step—and the guitars have a distinctly Greek, bouzouki-like resonance. It's all part of an observation about the love of a mysterious female, of course, a theme the band were slowly starting to abandon in favor of observational songs. Listening to "Girl," whether it's for the first or the 50th time, you find yourself hoping they would never entirely give up love balladry—and indeed the various Beatles did not, pursuing the theme—with varying degrees of success—throughout their band and solo careers. Note that their trademark sense of smutty humor was still present and correct despite the genuinely heartfelt nature of this song: you can hear them singing a backing line of "Tit, tit, tit," in the midsection, a fact confirmed by the musicians themselves on several occasions, the rascals.

3 I'm Looking Through You

When The Beatles wrote "I'm Looking Through You," they were clearly feeling more than a little peeved, exemplifying this with rudimentary organ stabs from Starr and an impassioned, top-of-the-register vocal from McCartney. "Love has a nasty habit of disappearing overnight", remarks McCartney with some venom, although the music motors along gently rather than hitting us with pyrotechnics. Once again, the song was about poor Jane Asher, the recipient of much of McCartney's compositional focus around this time, and once more, the atmosphere chez Asher must have been a little tense on the day *Rubber Soul* came out, eh?

4 In My Life

Wistful and with a maturity that belied his years, with "In My Life" Lennon came up with a song every bit the equal of McCartney's all-time career best, "Yesterday." Fixing his gaze on his Liverpudlian past, he is well supported by the contribution of George Martin, who imitates a harpsichord with his electric piano solo. McCartney plays his part well too, adding to the rich, nostalgic vocal layers, especially in the "All these places have their moments" section, in which he delivers an excellent high part. It's the message of the song that impacts most: without metaphor or opacity, Lennon recalls the emotions he felt, and continues to feel, as he looks back on the events of his sojourn on this plane . . . a lifespan which, as we now know to our grief, would be considerably shorter than he or anyone else expected.

5 Wait

In search of fresh musical pastures, The Beatles grabbed the chance with "Wait" to experiment on the backing track, with Starr, in particular, sounding as if he was finally enjoying his duties and adding some decorative drum fills. McCartney's bass drives the song along adroitly; he was now one of the absolute masters of his instrument, acknowledged in later years as a bass player who helped to

"'IN MY LIFE' WAS THE FIRST SONG THAT I WROTE THAT WAS REALLY, CONSCIOUSLY ABOUT MY LIFE."

JOHN LENNON

LEFT Baby, he can drive his car: the band congratulates John after he passes his driving test in February 1965.

ABOVE 1965 was a busy year for the band: two album releases, filming and promoting *Help!*, and European, US, and UK tours at the height of Beatlemania.

redefine the instrument's image completely. "Did I come back to your side?" asks Lennon in this song, a faintly hopeful paean to the joys of domestic reunions. Unusually for The Beatles, the song drags to a live-sounding ending rather than fading out or coming to a prearranged close: the raw and ready sixties as we knew them had finally arrived, in that sense.

6 If I Needed Someone

Taking its cue from a Byrds-like guitar phrasing, with Harrison doing his best Roger McGuinn impression, "If I Needed Someone" sounds a bit like a Beatles-influenced band improvising their way through a song that The Beatles might have written. The harmony "aahs" are here, the drum fills are enthusiastic rather than evolved, the bass springs effortlessly from octave to octave, and the luscious vocal layers are flawless. It's an underrated filler track, but one that deserves more attention.

7 Run for Your Life

After all that songwriting genius, "Run for Your Life" is a little underwhelming: the subject matter of chaotic love and its consequences has been covered many times before, and the music is energetic but a touch underpowered. Still, it detracts not from the mighty *Rubber Soul*, which still convinces the listener utterly thanks to the newfound maturity of the lyrics, in particular the wistful "In My Life" and the philosophical journey of "Norwegian Wood." The jocularity of the opening number, "Drive My Car," remains a welcome counterpoint to the musical depths of "Michelle" and "Girl," and the album transcends everything that went before it. Of course, even greater artistry was still to come.

ROOFTOP TOY BAND, CIRCA '64

ABOVE Larking about by the pool in LA during their North American tour, August 1964.

ABOVE An early promotional photo of the band with cartoon "Beatle" bodies.

PEEKING FROM THE DRESSING ROOM, MAY '63

GOOGLY-EYED GEORGE, MARCH '64

ABOVE The band meet Muhammad Ali (then Cassius Clay) during a visit to Malibu in February 1964.

BOBBY BEATLES, CIRCA '64

ABOVE Posing in pantomime costumes in 1963. Ringo as a bear, Paul as a cat, John as Ali Baba, and George as Robin Hood.

REVOLVER

Released **August 5, 1966**

The greatest album The Beatles ever made? It's wholly arguable, with every song a cultural landmark of its own.

··

SIDE ONE

1 Taxman

Surprisingly given The Beatles' reputation as peace lovers—but at the same time, understandably given their immense wealth—this album kicks off with George Harrison's savage indictment against the money grabbing practices of the British Inland Revenue, and specifically the high levels of tax levied on The Beatles' considerable investments. As Harrison so expertly explains in the song, Harold Wilson's government had decided in their infinite wisdom to claim 95 percent in tax of unearned revenue—in other words, investment income—above a certain limit. For working-class boys like The Beatles, who had worked hard for their money, this must have felt like a slap in the face in return for their efforts. Built around an insistent bass riff par excellence from McCartney—one which was later imitated by The Jam on their 1980 hit "Start!"—this song packs a sarcastic bite ("He'll tax the pennies on your eyes") and a truly searing guitar solo, this time from Paul McCartney,

> ## "I THINK IT'LL BE OUR BEST ALBUM YET. [T]HEY'LL NEVER BE ABLE TO COPY THIS!"
>
> ### PAUL McCARTNEY

LEFT In what would be their first and only live performance on the BBC's *Top of the Pops*, the band perform "Rain" and "Paperback Writer" in June 1966.

ABOVE Paul pictured as he arrives at EMI Studios, Abbey Road, for a rehearsal during the recording of *Revolver* in June 1966.

led punch. The slick, sharp funk of ng belies The Beatles' reputation ck or pop band; after "Taxman," nably placed at the top of *Revolver* for ery reason, it was obvious that there ery little music that they couldn't f they wished.

leanor Rigby

he downbeat subject matter of Eleanor Rigby" tells the demise of ly spinster. Full of depressingly lane, and therefore utterly real, lyrical ry ("darning his socks in the night," wiping the dirt from his hands"), ong's imaginative use of stringed uments gives it its heartbreaking gth. When accompanied by cellos, ns, and violas, the lyrics speak erfully, making for a fascinating rait of society—easily the equal of mporary real-life vignettes by bands as The Kinks. The refrain of "Ah, look l the lonely people," says it all: after anor Rigby," you'll consider the idea of age loneliness, now a modern public e, in a whole new light.

3 I'm Only Sleeping

This ode to the merits of indolence, as opposed to the stresses of the workaday world, is a bona fide leap forward—check out the reversed guitar parts, for example, which were genuinely tricky to pull off in those two-inch tape days. Then there's the guitar imitating a sitar, John Lennon's distinctive, unaffected vocal performance, and the general air of withdrawal from the real world, appropriately enough given The Beatles' inward gaze at this point in their lives. The sensibilities on display here signpost the Fab Four's immersion into—and influence on—the nascent British psychedelic scene. Countless bands would build an entire career out of this track, especially in the Britpop era. A high point is Harrison's guitar solo, recorded on two different tracks, each with different tones to confuse the ear. Can you imagine such a trick back in the "Can't Buy Me Love" days?

4 Love You To

The Beatles started the Western craze for the sitar in pop music, without a doubt, establishing the instrument as a different musical texture for the pop scene to

exploit in the name of broadening horizons. George Harrison arguably peaked as a sitar composer with this song, which is notable for its evocation of his worldview in a few short stanzas. "Each day goes by so fast," and "You can't hang a sign on me," he says, warning us that our Western worldview is pretty shallow. Thanks to The Beatles, music fans didn't have to stick to seeing the world in quite such traditional ways. The musicians from the Hindustani classical tradition who Harrison invited to play on the track included tabla and tambura players, leading to a veritable wall of sound that is all the more remarkable because Lennon and McCartney weren't involved. Can you imagine their reactions when they first heard it? "That's great, George—really interesting stuff there."

5 Here, There and Everywhere

You know, there are at least two ways to judge this sentimental song. On the one hand, it's a slow, emotional love ballad dripping with sentiment, loaded with sugary, mandolin-type guitar. On the other, it's an absolutely beautiful and inventive musical tableau, adorned with fabulous close harmonies—so your take on it is probably determined by the mood you're in on a given day. In either case, you can't disagree with its clean, lush textures and heartfelt dedication to the idea of timelessness, or indeed the multitude of studio trickery which went into its creation. Inspired by The Beach Boys' timeless "God Only Knows," this song's writer, McCartney, experimented with different tape speeds and adhered to no time signature at all for the opening lines, which set the tone before the band establishes a tempo. It sure is clever stuff, all right.

6 Yellow Submarine

This song has always been something of a conundrum. It's never really escaped the status of "cartoon singalong, sung by the drummer for a laugh," has it? But at the same time, The Beatles were known for their sense of humor, for their acid-drenched visuals, and for their appeal to children. Ringo Starr's vocal is perfect for the song, too, slightly flat as it

is, simply because a precision-engineered performance would have deadened the song, somehow. The comedy sound effects—nautical, mostly—are the only real irritants here, but then again, any song that you listen to five thousand times across a lifetime will become annoying after a while, right? We should really invoke classy references such as The Goon Show when considering "Yellow Submarine," as it does, after all, spring from the same surreal tradition.

7 She Said She Said

A fine example of precisely assembled psychedelia, "She Said, She Said" is a musically gripping and philosophically challenging track that reminds us once more that, by 1965, The Beatles were truly the masters of lyrical invention. Here, they concoct an uneasy atmosphere that complements Lennon's lyrics, inspired by the experience of "ego loss"—not something

we recommend, friends—during an acid trip with the *Easy Rider* actor Peter Fonda. "I know what it's like to be dead," is the key line, which sounds like a bit of whimsy until you find out that it was meant seriously at the time. Imagine being a fly on the wall at *that* party . . . and less threateningly, have you ever witnessed a better drumming performance from Ringo than this song?

SIDE TWO

1 Good Day Sunshine

An eternal feel-good song, "Good Day Sunshine" captures a particularly hot day at John Lennon's mansion. The interplay between the jaunty vocals from Paul McCartney and the rolling piano courtesy of George Martin is particularly impressive, but it's that sunny chorus that infects the listener most. Make no mistake, though, ➥

ABOVE John, George, and Paul pictured in the studio while recording parts for the *Yellow Submarine* film. Their characters' voices in the film were provided by actors, however.

RIGHT "Yellow Submarine" became the basis for The Beatles' fourth film in 1968, though the band were disillusioned with their contractual film obligations by that point.

those expert, almost casual verse vocals slip smoothly along, barely accompanied by a song structure, with hints of chords underneath the mid-register vocals. What's great about this song is its sudden leap into the chorus pyrotechnics after the lazy lope of the verse: another masterpiece of the arranger's art. After the barely disguised darkness at the heart of the songs on *Revolver*'s first side, were we to be treated to a lighter experience on the flip? Perhaps, listeners, perhaps.

2 And Your Bird Can Sing

Now, this song is genuinely uplifting, thanks to its ascending chorus line, but spiritually, "And Your Bird Can Sing" is closer to the material on *Rubber Soul*. It doesn't quite have the depth of, say, "Tomorrow Never Knows"—but then, what song does?—leading Lennon to dismiss it as a throwaway composition. To most reasonable ears, that's a little unfair: after all, just because a song is cheerful that doesn't mean it lacks value. Indeed, when you assess *Revolver* as a whole, it's these lighter moments that make the more thoughtful songs seem even darker—and both songwriting methods win out as a result. Unconfirmed theories suggest that this song was aimed at, or inspired by, Frank Sinatra, whose good fortune was, the lyrics obliquely hinted, no guarantee that he could wholly appreciate the nuances of life.

3 For No One

Documenting the end of McCartney's relationship ("A love that should have lasted years") with actress Jane Asher, this classy little number is improved immeasurably

"I SUPPOSE IF I HAD SAID TELEVISION WAS MORE POPULAR THAN JESUS, I WOULD HAVE GOT AWAY WITH IT."

JOHN LENNON

by the addition of a majestic French horn solo, included at the suggestion of producer and fifth Beatle George Martin. The song is competent and polished, but it took the inclusion of the classical instrument to elevate it to a truly extraordinary level. McCartney's vocal doesn't overdo the emotion, which some listeners find a little unusual given the song's personal nature—but isn't that how real-life breakups so often happen? A couple tire of each other and walk numbly away, waiting for something better to come along.

4 Doctor Robert

Now, rock 'n' roll legend has it that the subject of "Doctor Robert" was Dr. Robert Freymann, a physician of popular choice who would happily administer various substances when requested to do so by "tired" socialites and rock stars on New York's elite arts scene. What these substances might be depended, so it is reported, on whether a given "patient" was suffering from the ill effects of too much partying, or whether they required treatment for full-blown addiction. However, it is thought that a concoction of vitamin B12 and methamphetamine might well have been the most popular prescription. The song is memorable for Lennon's vocal attack, the gutsy backing vocals from McCartney, and the effective blend of guitar and sitar. "Doctor Robert" would also inspire a *nom de guerre* for the lead singer of the eighties pop act Blow Monkeys, trivia enthusiasts.

LEFT In 1966, John's notorious "more popular than Jesus" remark led to angry backlash in America, overshadowing both *Revolver*'s release and the band's 1966 US tour.

ABOVE The band watch as George has a sitar lesson during their first trip to India in July 1966. Later that year, Harrison returned to India to study sitar under the legendary Ravi Shankar.

5 I Want to Tell You

This song typifies the continued transition of The Beatles, as it documents the continued emergence of George Harrison as a powerful songwriter. Although he couldn't possibly be as prolific as Lennon or McCartney, when he wrote songs, people wanted to listen to them. To that end, lyrically "I Want to Tell You" is a catalogue of all the thoughts that Harrison was unable to articulate—and which required him to spend time striving for alternatives in different religions. The composition benefits from a nagging hookline that accelerates on the chorus and is accompanied by an off-kilter piano. Soon, he would reach even greater heights as a writer: great moments lay ahead for The Quiet One.

6 Got to Get You into My Life

Ah, Mary Jane! The Beatles—and McCartney in particular—were fond of their "jazz cigarettes," and this song's alleged espousal of the delights of marijuana is wisely concealed behind what seems to be a straightforward love song. The tune is driven along by brass arrangements courtesy of Georgie Fame's Blue Flames, and there's some climactic guitar playing from Harrison, which made it ripe for later interpretation by Cliff Bennett and his Rebel Rousers. This song is a rowdy, old-school rhythm and blues workout—a fully-leaded anthem of the sort that "blues shouters" of the old guard had made so popular in the fifties. When The Beatles attempted any musical genre at this point, they tended to pull it off with aplomb, and there is no finer example than this.

7 Tomorrow Never Knows

Now here's a real left turn at the traffic lights—and one of the reasons why many Beatles fans think that *Revolver* is a better album than the obvious masterpiece, Sgt. Pepper. "Tomorrow Never Knows" is the furthest foray to date by The Beatles into the psychedelic third eye. Everything about "Tomorrow Never Knows" was revolutionary, from the compressed drums, the squiggly tape loops, the run-backwards guitars, and the utter "otherness" of Lennon's treated vocals. All this in combination was guaranteed to make your jaw drop in wonderment—or in the case of the teenyboppers of the late sixties, in utter disbelief. Musically and in production terms, this song represents a seismic change, and one that can still be felt today. Nothing about the earlier, muscular R&B of "Taxman" et al. could prepare the unenlightened for this Technicolor finale. The case for *Revolver* being a more advanced body of work than Sgt. Pepper is largely based on this lysergic climax.

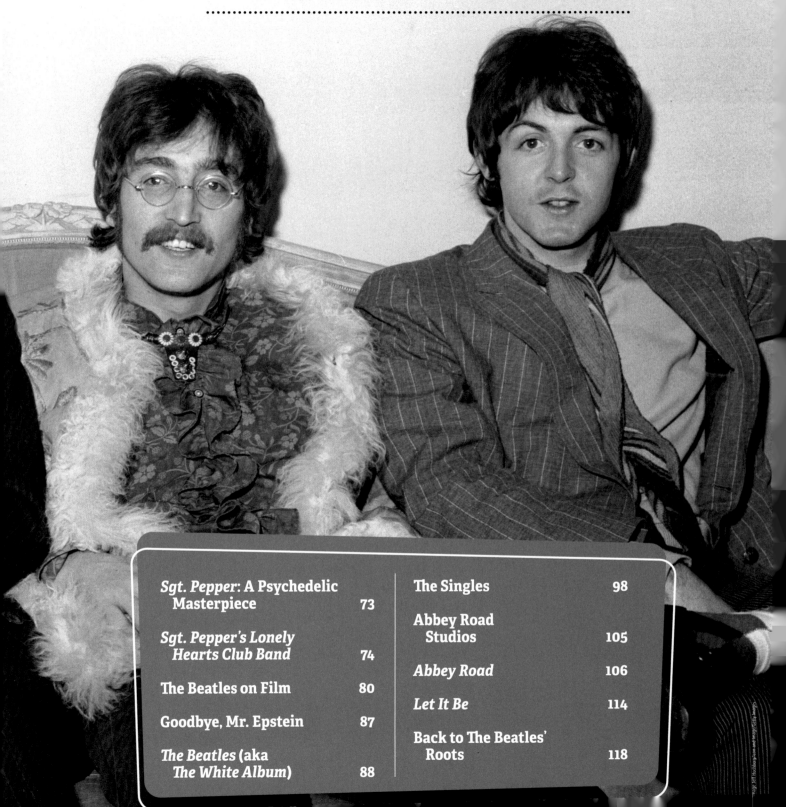

THE STUDIO YEARS

NE

The Beatles embraced their alter egos to help break away from their established image.

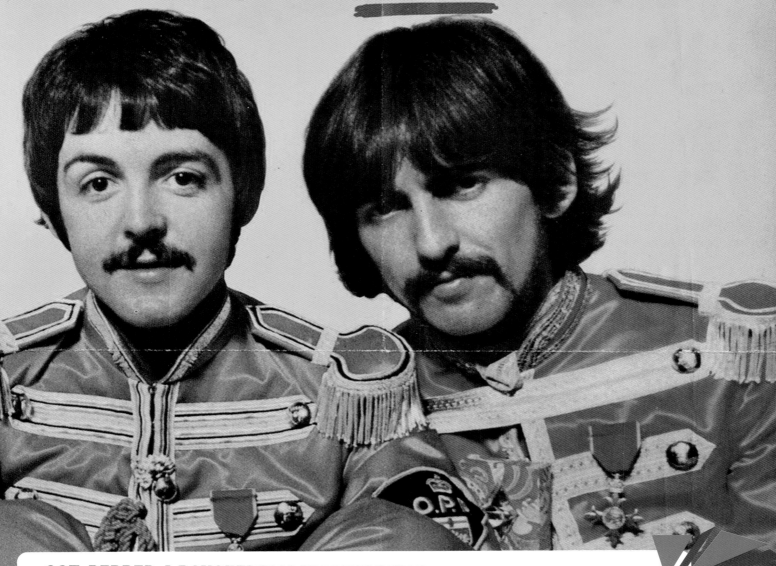

HEARTS CLUB BAND
BEATLES LP HERE NOW

SGT. PEPPER: A PSYCHEDELIC MASTERPIECE

There is no accurate way of describing British culture of the sixties without mentioning *Sgt. Pepper's Lonely Hearts Club Band*, the album which defined 1967 as the Summer of Love and which ushered in a whole new way of drug assisted, otherworldly thinking.

Before fans even placed the LP on their turntable, they were obliged to assimilate the unique cover artwork by artist Peter Blake, which featured dozens of celebrities that The Beatles admired or found influential, and the inner sleeve art itself, which showed the band in their instantly iconic *Sgt. Pepper* uniforms. It was McCartney who first came up with the band-within-a-band concept. "We were fed up with being The Beatles," he explained. "I thought, let's not be ourselves. Let's develop alter egos."

The album proved to be a head-spinning experience. Old-school music-hall songs abounded ("Being for the Benefit of Mr. Kite!"); psychedelic wig outs were beautifully opaque ("Lucy in the Sky with Diamonds"); Indian mysticism reared its head ("Within You Without You); and technological experimentation messed with the most together of heads (the ending of "A Day in the Life"). It would take thousands of words to even begin to explain this album. Go and listen to it, one more time.

SGT. PEPPER'S LONELY HEARTS CLUB BAND

Released **May 26, 1967**

The greatest album of all time? A lot of people think so.
Let's examine the evidence.

SIDE ONE

1 Sgt. Pepper's Lonely Hearts Club Band

This immortal album opener kicks off with a snatch of an orchestra tuning up in the pit, with McCartney playing the part of master of ceremonies ("The singer's gonna sing a song!") of this imagined event in some bastion of the establishment—we're thinking of the Royal Albert Hall, although admittedly that may be because the RAH is mentioned later in the album. This piece of ambient scene setting is followed rapidly by some chunky rock guitar and Ringo's thudding drums. With this highly creative direction, The Beatles adopted the guise of one of rock's most famous alter egos, Sgt. Pepper himself, who—with his Lonely Hearts Club Band—personified the mother of all musical concepts. Only The Beatles themselves would know who the good sergeant was based on, but we're betting he had an impressive moustache.

2 With a Little Help from My Friends

Every Beatles album needs a Ringo-sung song for comic relief, and this is it, segued neatly in after the opening cut with the sound of fans baying for The Beatles, recorded at the Hollywood Bowl. Now, the song structure of "With a Little Help from My Friends" may be based on a slightly cheesy call-and-response structure, but the naïvely utopian message of mutual support and Ringo's surprisingly endearing nasal delivery still appeal. There's also some "Beatle and Butt-Head" humor in the form of the tricky question "What do you see when you turn out the light?" to which the logical answer should surely be "Nothing, because it's dark"—but which Ringo actually answers with "I can't tell you, but I know it's mine."

3 Lucy in the Sky with Diamonds

Is there any more knowingly hallucinogenic opening line than "Picture yourself in a boat on a river with tangerine trees and marmalade skies"? It's little wonder that the easily excited music fans of this world soon spotted that the initials of this track spelled out LSD. The truth was far more innocent, as the title had been based on a drawing by Lennon's son Julian. Still, the connection is an easy one to make, as the listener is assailed with fantastical imagery ("Cellophane flowers of yellow and green towering over your head") and those unmistakable organ-driven atmospherics, the latter created when a Lowrey electric organ was manipulated in the studio to sound very trippy indeed. This song is essentially the world of Lewis Carroll made real in aural form, and while that world may not necessarily be a place you'd like to inhabit full time, there's no harm in dropping in, turning on, and flipping out for a while.

4 Getting Better

There's a lot more to this song, often relegated to the status of simple rocker when compared to the mind-blowing psych-outs of the better-known tracks, than simple optimism. Dig deep and you'll see signs of Lennon versus McCartney, with the former sarcastically riposting "It can't get no worse," when the latter warbles, ➤

THE band pictured at the press party to celebrate the upcoming release of Sgt. Pepper in May 1967. The event was hosted at Brian Epstein's home.

audience, now understand perfectly. This is the fact that for the generation who had fought and died in the Second World War, a lifetime of security and stability was exactly what they wanted after the horrors of that conflict. On the other hand, their kids—born during or after the war—just wanted to take drugs, listen to rock music, and protest against the establishment. Neither side would ever understand the other, leading to commonplace family schisms such as the one depicted so accurately in this song.

7 Being for the Benefit of Mr. Kite!

You can almost smell the sawdust and elephant dung emanating from this fairground production, based on an old Victorian circus poster acquired by Lennon from an antique shop. His treated vocal provides a fabulous account of the delights on offer from the celebrated Mr. K of the title, but it's the soundscape that George Martin created from an amalgam of Victorian instrumentation—such as steam organs and harmoniums—that is the real winner here. Now, it's only fair to say that this song becomes a little jarring after several listens, thanks to Lennon's frankly unnerving vocals and the fairground melodies, but as a piece of studio work, it's incomparable. Remember, if you want the sound of a lion roaring or a monkey chattering nowadays, you only have to click a mouse; back then, you literally had to go to a zoo and hold a microphone up outside a given beastie's cage. And yet The Beatles and Martin got it done, and done incredibly well.

SIDE TWO

1 Within You Without You

"What's happened to George?" screamed the teenyboppers. "He's gone all weird and mystical." Well, they were wrong: "Within You Without You" was indeed mistakenly

"It's getting better all the time," and something of a confessional from Lennon when he sings, "I used to be cruel to my woman." As we now know, the late genius was occasionally violent to his partners throughout his life: was he apologizing for his behavior here, albeit in a rather underhand manner?

5 Fixing a Hole

Sure, the line "I'm fixing a hole where the rain gets in, that stops my mind from wandering" has a dreamlike quality. It had theorists speculating about a mystical third eye on the part of the singer, or even a magical wormhole through space that allowed The Beatles to fly into worlds unknown. In actual fact the hole in question was inspired by something rather more prosaic—the leaky roof of McCartney's Scottish farmhouse. Clever lad that he is, he expands on the metaphor to express his wish that his thinking could be free of its usual boundaries and fly

wherever it wants. Perhaps those theorists were on to something after all. Whatever the intent, this is a rather beautiful song that lies squarely on the expert vocal hooks ("where it will go-oo-ooo," and so on), delivered in McCartney's wonderfully clean mid-register voice.

6 She's Leaving Home

Like "Eleanor Rigby," which preceded this song thematically on the *Revolver* album, real-life concerns—in this case, the post-war generation gap between parents and their siblings—were brought to life in this song in full, heartbreaking detail. We're presented with several sides to the story of a girl who departs her oppressive background, going to meet "a man from the motor trade," most poignantly bearing witness to the grieving of her abandoned parents. "We gave her everything money could buy," they wail, failing to grasp the point that we, an educated

TO this day, Sgt. Pepper remains the best-selling studio album of all time in the UK, and has sold over 32 million copies worldwide.

> **"IT WON'T BE THE BEATLES, IT'LL BE THIS OTHER BAND, SO WE'LL BE ABLE TO LOSE OUR IDENTITIES IN THIS."**
>
> PAUL McCARTNEY

viewed in this way by a number of out-of-touch Beatles followers, such was its departure from the group's staple fare. It is, however, the logical extension of the musical tutelage which Harrison had received from the Indian sitar master, Ravi Shankar. Its lyrical theme, a rally against money grabbing consumerism, was often revisited in Harrison's later contributions to the group's catalogue, as well as in his solo career—even if he was also highly regarded for his anti-government protest, "Taxman," from *Revolver*. Harrison was truly a man of many facets.

2 When I'm Sixty-Four

This bizarre album never, but never, settles into a single musical style. As a demonstration of The Beatles' versatility, "When I'm Sixty-Four" is nothing less than a witty exploration of the travails of old age, expressed through a vaudeville turn of phrase that harks back to the days of music hall. The clarinet lines deliver a perfect 1930s vibe, while the rootsy bass and more-or-less absent guitars take the

song a long step away from the basic rock structure of some of the other tracks. Like "She's Leaving Home," "When I'm Sixty-Four" also flips the listener's expectations by narrating an older person's point of view—in this case an old couple.

3 Lovely Rita

A rousing, upbeat song, "Lovely Rita" celebrates the mundane and everyday in life—in particular, the lives of people who were the salt of the earth, as beloved by Paul McCartney, and rather less so by John Lennon. In this case, the humble parking meter maid Rita is the subject, and in keeping with the "love thy neighbor" spirit of the times, the song is sympathetic to her plight. After a clumsy attempt to seduce the

song's heroine ("Took her home, I nearly made it / Sitting on the sofa with a sister or two"), which is played out against a prominent walking bass line, the narrator settles into a general admiration of her beauty, accompanied by soaring, dreamlike vocal harmonies. Even the slightly forced jocularity of McCartney's vocal delivery has a certain appeal.

4 Good Morning Good Morning

Outwardly, "Good Morning Good Morning" appears to be a feel-good pop number. Delve a little deeper into the lyrical content, however, and the song reveals itself as a classic Lennon sneer against the everyday conventions of the workaday world. Starting brightly with a burst of cockerel and stabs of compressed brass, the song begins its message of light despair, talking ⏩

Images John Pratt/Keystone/Hulton Archive/Getty Images (Linda);
Michael Ochs Archives/Getty Images (portrait); Dan Moss/Alamy (Harrison)

about having "nothing to do" and everything being closed down, "like a ruin." It's a depressingly familiar tale of modern life, and as such plays an admirable role by establishing a grey background against which the Day-Glo, psychedelic songs that follow glisten all the more vividly.

5 Sgt. Pepper's Lonely Hearts Club Band (Reprise)

The first sign that the *Sgt. Pepper* album is going to end on a psychotically deranged blaze of musical color comes at the start of this "Reprise" of the main theme. Don't be fooled into thinking that this short snippet is a lesser version of the earlier song: it is compressed into a deadly effective reiteration, that's all. That unmistakable two-note guitar lick at the beginning is like an air raid warning, with a nervous background click, McCartney's supremely cocky "One-a-two-a-three-a-foh!", some unnerving audience rumble, and the funkiest snatch of drums that Ringo Starr ever recorded. The band then comes in, playing a single chord in unison, and in doing so making two guitars and a bass sound apocalyptically heavy, helped by the reverb on the vocals that follow. Keep an ear out for the nifty "one and only Lonely Hearts Club Band," and the warning of "It's getting very near the end." After a wail, a whoop, and a final chord, we're left with the ultimate outro to any album.

TOP John, Ringo, and Paul rehearsing on pianos at Abbey Road Studios, circa 1967. George is seated in the background.

ABOVE McCartney conducts the 40-piece orchestra for "A Day in the Life." "We all felt a sense of occasion," recalled George Martin. "It was the largest orchestra we ever used on a Beatles recording."

6 A Day in the Life

A truly mind-bending performance, there is so much in "A Day in the Life" to applaud and admire that it's easy to forget that it is essentially the melding together of two entirely separate compositions. First, we're given Lennon's floating vocal performance on the opening segment: he sadly tells us "He blew his mind out in a car," referencing the tragic death of The Beatles' friend and socialite, Tara Browne. He then focuses on the day-to-day absurdities of the media world, referring to a newspaper headline about four thousand holes found in Blackburn, Lancashire, before the song segues into McCartney's countercultural

"Found my way upstairs and had a smoke" lyrics—even if the smoke he was referring to was nothing stronger than a Woodbine cigarette.

Sgt. Pepper's Lonely Hearts Club Band comes rolling to a close with a terrifying ascending orchestra, marked out by the distant ping of an alarm clock, followed by an immense piano chord, reverbed and rebooted to make it last minutes. Finally, there is the infinite groove—a literal one in the case of the vinyl LP—that shocked the listener with three seconds of repeating gibberish. No wonder this album spawned so many prog-rock concept LPs in the late sixties and early seventies. It was the first

album to come as a complete package—right down to Peter Blake's iconic cover artwork and the Technicolor Pepper costumes.

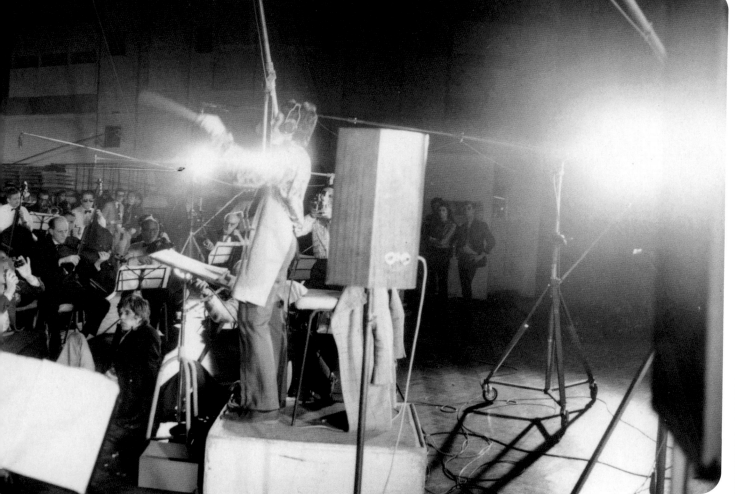

THE BEATLES ON FILM

When Beatlemania hit, the silver screen beckoned! Let's take a look at the best of The Beatles' movie career.

STARR, Lennon, Harrison, and McCartney enjoyed success on screen, both as a band and in various solo projects.

A HARD DAY'S NIGHT
RELEASED JULY 1964

Young, energetic, and cheerfully riding a massive wave of popularity like no new band before or since, The Beatles seemed to be a happy bunch in *A Hard Day's Night*. The "story" was paper-thin, involving a chaotic sequence of events in which the four musicians try to avoid doing what they're told by their manager and other orbiting handlers. Notable actors include Wilfrid "Steptoe" Brambell as Paul's supposed grandfather, and Norman Rossington as the band's manager, however, this slight but amusing film really belongs to The Beatles themselves.

The film isn't enjoyable so much because of its plot—in which the band finally wins the day and plays a show to an adoring bunch of fans, before being airlifted to their next gig—but because of the airtime afforded to the musicians themselves, and because of its amazing music. After the title track announces the film, The Beatles spin through "I Should Have Known Better," before we're treated to excerpts of "I Wanna Be Your Man," the Harrison-penned "Don't Bother Me," and then "All My Loving," one of the best pre-*Revolver* love songs from the early catalogue. A phenomenal rendition of

THE Fab Four's first feature film proved to be a critical and commercial success.

"Can't Buy Me Love" is followed by "And I Love Her," while "If I Fell" is played and later reprised.

A triumphant victory lap of "She Loves You" winds up the film, leaving the audience thoroughly introduced to the young band's early songs. It could have all ended there, you know: who knew back in '64 if there would be another visual document of the Fab Four after this one?

HELP! saw the band travel across the world to try and protect Ringo from a nefarious cult.

HELP!
RELEASED JULY 1965

Although *Help!* was released in theaters a year after *A Hard Day's Night*, and doesn't enjoy the same level of appreciation as its predecessor, it's the more enjoyable film in some ways. The plot, while hardly Orson Welles-like in depth, is a little less predictable than that of *AHDN*, and the direction—once again from Richard Lester—is a touch more ambitious.

This time around, there's one of Alfred Hitchcock's infamous MacGuffins, a ring belonging to Ringo (you see what they did there?) that is sought by an unidentified Eastern cult. An exotic chase through Switzerland, Buckingham Palace, and the Bahamas—a consequence of Lester's increased budget this time—leads to the final showdown and the expected cheery denouement.

Look, no one was expecting a cinematic

epic from the Fab Four at this point, and indeed this is a throwaway movie, a bit of a laugh for the fans and a chance for Ringo Starr—always the clown of the group—to enjoy the limelight for a change. Where the film excels is in its soundtrack, a glorious run-through of the best of their early-middle (or late-early) career. The song "Help!" was written by Lennon after the film title was confirmed, while the bittersweet "You're Going to Lose That Girl," and the downright heartbreaking "You've Got to Hide Your Love Away" add depth right from the off.

Other musical highlights include a terrific run-through of "The Night Before," in which fragments of "She's a Woman" appear, alongside a bizarre Indian version of "A Hard Day's Night," retitled "Another Hard Day's Night" for the soundtrack album. Oh, and make sure you check out the instrumental version of "From Me to You," from the ring-stealing scene . . . it's pure sixties whimsy.

LONDON PAVILION

THE BEATLES

IN THEIR FIRST FULL LENGTH,
HILARIOUS, ACTION—PACKED FILM!

A HARD
DAY'S NIGHT

12 SMASH SONG—HITS!

A Hard Day's Night was made on a budget of about 500,000 dollars, but took over 11 million dollars at the box office.

HALF-WEIGHT
Hush Puppies
IN BRUSHED PIGSKIN
ALWAYS STAY SMART!

PEDESTRIANS

"I WAS TRYING TO THINK OF THE PEOPLE THAT I MEET IN A DAY THAT AREN'T ACTING IN SOME WAY, AND OF COURSE I'M ACTING, YOU KNOW, ALL THE TIME."

PAUL MCCARTNEY

MAGICAL MYSTERY TOUR
RELEASED DECEMBER 1967

As with all The Beatles' filmed efforts, 1967's *Magical Mystery Tour* was a friendly but amateurish movie project redeemed by amazing music. Shot in such poor quality that a decent print didn't exist for decades, the film follows the band and sundry friends on a bus tour through various locales, and while there's a certain amount of enjoyment to be derived from the action if you're a true disciple, it's probably best not to attempt a rigorous critical analysis.

Still, there's the music—and what music it is. In order, the songs to which the viewer is treated kick off with the rarely bettered title cut, with those ambitious sound effects, demonstrating that in the absence of Brian Epstein, The Beatles could still push out the sonic envelope. Then there's "The Fool on the Hill," in which McCartney's vocals sound languid in their interplay with the revolving harmonies: together with the delightful recorder-like flute on the instrumental break, it's something of a musical triumph.

The band performs "Your Mother Should Know" for *The Magical Mystery Tour*'s colorful finale.

A version of "She Loves You"—after only four years, sounding like the work of a completely different band—is here, played on a fairground organ as part of the general medley of background music during the race scene. There's an instrumental number, "Flying," played on Lennon's Mellotron, and a rendition of "All My Loving," orchestrated in the style of the *pas de deux* section of Tchaikovsky's Nutcracker ballet.

If all that isn't avant-garde enough for you, raise a glass to "I am the Walrus," still the most surreal song ever written. Lennon's ultimate stream of fancy encapsulates everything from icky playground nonsense ("Yellow matter custard dripping from a dead dog's eye") to his anger against the stuffiness of English institutions. It's still a profoundly unusual song, all these years later, poor covers by bands such as Oasis having failed to reduce its impact.

What remains? There's "Jessie's Dream," an instrumental that was not released on any other official audio recording, and the excellent "Blue Jay Way" from Harrison, and eerie, creeping song. "Death Cab for Cutie" is then performed by the Bonzo Dog Doo-Dah Band, in a break from The Beatles' psychological whimsy, before we call it a night with "Your Mother Should Know," a classic McCartney exercise in music-hall nostalgia. This song is perhaps best heard in the context of the film's visuals rather than as a standalone composition, it has to be said.

"Magical Mystery Tour (Reprise)" and a section of "Hello, Goodbye" see this slightly bizarre, not wholly successful film out, leaving the viewer slightly dazed by it all, if also reminded how accomplished the music is.

LEFT The Beatles weren't initially fans of the US cartoon about them, which put them off participating more in *Yellow Submarine*.

ABOVE The *Reel Music* compilation featured a selection of songs that featured in the band's films.

YELLOW SUBMARINE

RELEASED JULY 1968

As twentieth-century animated films go, *Yellow Submarine* is less conservative than *Dumbo* and less groundbreaking than *Fantasia*—but at the same time, it epitomizes something about its year of release than either of those big-studio classics. Naïve, psychedelic, and slightly disturbing, the movie combined childlike innocence with fairytale threat, and is best seen with critical faculties disengaged.

The music, however, has more substance than you might expect from the visuals. The title track is pure McCartney, although he is said to have had some help from The Beatles' chum Donovan on the line "Sky of blue, sea of green." There is a multitude of nautical sound effects courtesy of Brian Jones of The Rolling Stones, among others. Another high point is "Hey Bulldog," a raw blues rocker that features an amusing howling dog section and an effective bassline.

The music often references the content, rather than simply being bolted onto the visuals. For example, "It's All Too Much," which feels awash in LSD, is a high-water mark of British psychedelia, from the droned guitar introduction and sea of feedback to the very English obsession of "making it home in time for tea."

"Pepperland" presents us with a sweeping vista of violins, cellos, piano, and harp, evoking the idyllic fantasyland of Pepper before the attack of the film's antagonists, the Blue Meanies.

Visual and musical references abound. For instance, In "Sea of Time," we're treated to the line, "Look, the hands are slowing down," from the voice of cartoon McCartney: this cues up a spellbinding swirl of eerie George Martin-led orchestration to depict the fact that someone is messing about with the hands of time. Furthermore, our descent into the "Sea of Monsters" comes replete with sinister brass as a counterpoint to the bursts of the familiar signature tune.

Critics didn't really know how to approach the soundtrack on its release, and indeed it's difficult to appraise today because the art direction is so unusual, let alone the film's context in the anything-goes era of psychedelia. Some more hard-hearted writers have deemed Harrison's "Only a Northern Song" as nothing more than a reject ("You may think the chords are going wrong") from *Sgt. Pepper*, but that's unfair. Similarly, "All You Need Is Love" is venerated for its historical ramifications, thanks to the global satellite linkup of the *Our World* live TV broadcast in 1967, but its appearance here outside of the context of the film storyline is a touch incongruous.

Yellow Submarine was credited with elevating the status of animation to something more than just children's entertainment.

It's not all perfect—"All Together Now" is a singalong with all the charm of a football chant, although mercifully it's all over quickly before any real pain sets in—but *Yellow Submarine*'s reputation as a patchwork of Beatles leftovers is undeserved. Yes, it is something of a cash-in LP—see the sidelong addition of soundtrack orchestral works from George Martin—but no suite of songs with psychedelic nuggets such as "It's All Too Much" and "Only a Northern Song" should be judged too harshly.

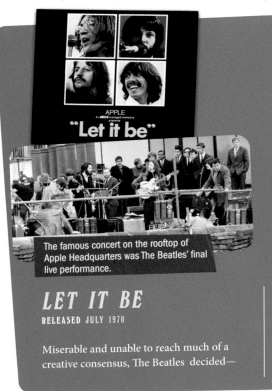

The famous concert on the rooftop of Apple Headquarters was The Beatles' final live performance.

LET IT BE

RELEASED JULY 1970

Miserable and unable to reach much of a creative consensus, The Beatles decided— perhaps against their better instincts—to record t hemselves jamming in the studio in 1969. A surprisingly large number of songs appeared in the resulting documentary film *Let It Be*, although many of them had been heard before. Viewing the band from inside the studio, we're given a perspective that is irresistible, despite the bad vibes and awkwardness: seeing how these great creative minds worked in sync—or not, as the case might be—was a treat that no one expected back in the pre-reality TV days.

Without running through all of the 26 or so complete or fragmented songs here, let's point out the high and low musical points of this unusual movie. "Paul's Piano Intro," which is based on "Adiago for Strings" by Samuel Barber, is a reminder that McCartney could do high culture when he chose, and a later piece called "Jazz Piano Song" is a lesser, if equally enjoyable hint at the wide-ranging music that would follow from the bass player. Versions of album cuts such as "Oh! Darling" and the immortal "Across the Universe" are sublime, while a run-through of "Octopus's Garden" gives us a moment of light relief—which is much needed, believe us.

Elsewhere, you'll enjoy a cover of Smokey Robinson's classic "You've Really Got a Hold on Me," and a languid spin through the lovely "The Long and Winding Road," but for many fans, this film truly excels when The Beatles roar through a rock 'n' roll medley and the years of strife briefly fall away. "Rip It Up," "Shake, Rattle and Roll," "Kansas City," "Miss Ann," and an immense "Lawdy Miss Clawdy" remind us, rather sadly in retrospect, what a powerful band The Beatles had been when they were young and optimistic.

"Let It Be" and a slick version of "Get Back" round off this slightly uncomfortable film— and as the credits roll, there's something of a death knell in the air for The Beatles. This film was their farewell.

GEORGE, John, and Paul pictured with Brian Epstein at the Our World event on June 25, 1967, just a few weeks before Epstein's untimely death.

GOODBYE, MR. EPSTEIN

The importance of Brian Epstein to the careers of The Beatles should not be understated, even if he only managed them for the first half of their existence as a band. He first played a part in their lives in 1962, having learned something about the music industry from his family's Liverpool record shop, NEMS, and remained with them until 1967, when he succumbed on August 27, to a combination of sleeping pills and alcohol. His death was ruled accidental, but rumors of suicide have never gone away.

As a manager, Epstein made few errors—although those he made tended to cost The Beatles dearly—and the band learned much about the business from him. After his death, Paul McCartney gradually rose to a position of leadership within the band, determined not to let their progress be derailed. The Beatles' former de facto leader, John Lennon, was mired in his own problems in the late sixties, chiefly a heroin addiction.

As the band's dynamic changed, so did their fortunes, eventually splitting in 1970—at least partly due to the role of Epstein's successor, Allen Klein. Who knows what would have happened had Epstein survived that overdose?

THE BEATLES
(AKA *THE WHITE ALBUM*)

Released **November 22, 1968**

Double albums are always either a blessing or a curse. In the case of The Beatles' self-titled epic, which was it to be?

The BEATLES

SIDE ONE

1 Back in the U.S.S.R.
Paul McCartney's playful tribute to The Beach Boys kicks off with the upsurge of a jet plane taking off, before sending the listener careering headlong into pun-filled lyrics set in Cold War Soviet Union. Buoyed as it is with excellent guitar work from Lennon, Harrison, and the versatile bassist himself, the song never once threatens to lapse into parody, because it's so good in its own right. The hilarity of the "woo-ee-oo" backing vocals from Harrison and Lennon, in glorious falsetto, are enough to make this song a known classic, and proof that The Beatles feared nothing and no one. Who would dare to arrest them for pro-Soviet propaganda? Exactly.

2 Dear Prudence
Apparently constructed of sheer languidity, this Lennon-penned number was designed to coax Mia Farrow's sister Prudence out of her meditative state, with its "Won't you come out to play" and "daisy chain" lyrics. It's a slow-burning psychedelic gem that plays out to a wonderful climax of Indian guitar phrasing from Harrison, tinkling piano from McCartney, and a slightly sinister backing vocal drone of "Look around, round" from none other than Beatle roadie Mal Evans. A very successful cover version by goths Siouxsie & The Banshees in 1983 added a spooky edge that actually suited the composition down to the ground, making this already slightly dark song into a much more threatening one.

3 Glass Onion
With McCartney's bass tones well to the fore, "Glass Onion" boasts an impassioned, somewhat sarcastic Lennon vocal that taunts the obsessive fan with an unraveling of The Beatles' fairly recent past of the *Magical Mystery Tour*, as evidenced by the "Walrus was Paul" line. Extra textures include some amateurish recorder from said Walrus and a creepy orchestral denouement, but Lennon's surrealist riddles win the day.

4 Ob-La-Di, Ob-La-Da
Love or hate this strange song, it's proof that once again, The Beatles wanted this album to be made up of multiple genres of music. There is a clear trajectory from the sublimeness of "Dear Prudence" to the ridiculousness of "Ob-La-Di, Ob-La-Da," a cod-Jamaican, ska-flavored number. Fortunately for the many listeners who love its bumptious attitude, this jaunty tune quickly becomes ingrained in the subconscious, as those Scottish opportunists Marmalade were quick to recognize with a big hit in '68.

5 Wild Honey Pie
This is a mere song snippet, clocking in at a brief 52 seconds, and is best viewed as a piece of Beatle self-indulgence—a throwaway singalong comprised of nothing more than repetitive, falsetto wails of "Honey Pie." Sure, it doesn't really bear serious analysis at this point, but who else was recording songs as stubbornly experimental as this at the time?

6 The Continuing Story of Bungalow Bill
After its Spanish-sounding opening, this popular—if opaque—song finds Lennon singing comedic lyrics in the style of a small child in the buildup to the chorus, which soon accelerates into the familiar, arms-in-the-air singalong. It also features Ringo Starr's then-wife Maureen and Yoko Ono, with swathes of rattling tambourine and Mellotron. As such, it's best regarded as a curio for devoted fans. »

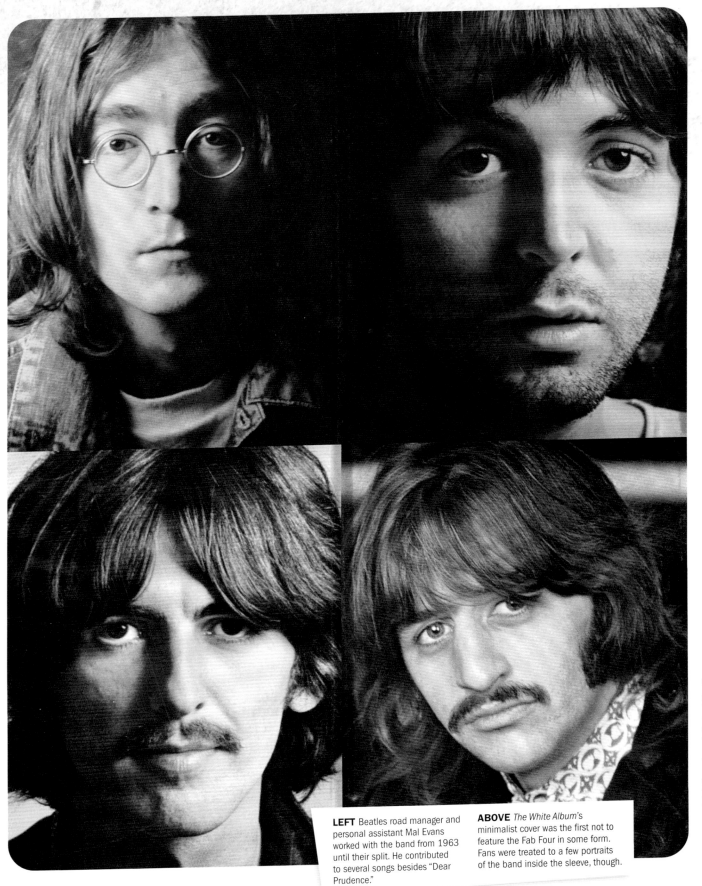

Words: Joel McIver. Images: The Beatles (album cover); sleeve-x-foto/Alamy (portraits); Estate Of Keith Morris/Redferns/Getty Images (Mal Evans)

LEFT Beatles road manager and personal assistant Mal Evans worked with the band from 1963 until their split. He contributed to several songs besides "Dear Prudence."

ABOVE *The White Album*'s minimalist cover was the first not to feature the Fab Four in some form. Fans were treated to a few portraits of the band inside the sleeve, though.

89

Many of the album's tracks were written during the band's trip to India in 1968 where they studied transcendental meditation under the Maharishi Mahesh Yogi.

7 While My Guitar Gently Weeps

This song is a bona fide classic, and has received a renewed lease of life in the last couple of years thanks to an astounding live version, viewable online, with the sadly late Prince tearing it up on lead guitar. The original "While My Guitar Gently Weeps" is aided by a guitar solo from the blues god and friend of songwriter Harrison, Eric Clapton. Slowhand's presence sees The Beatles on their very best musical form—with Starr's urgent drums, McCartney's economical piano and bass, and Lennon rising to the challenge on guitar. Possibly the best backing band in the world ever?

8 Happiness Is a Warm Gun

Progressive rock begins here, with this song the sound of The Beatles as a true band, displaying their chops in various different idioms—folk, rock, and even doo-wop among them. Featuring as it does some of Lennon's most vivid lyrical imagery—"The man with the multicolored mirrors on his hobnail boots"—the song is a creative tour

> ## "IT'S PRETTY HARD TRYING TO FIT THREE GUYS' MUSIC ONTO ONE ALBUM—THAT'S WHY WE DID A DOUBLE."
>
> **JOHN LENNON**

de force. Check the vocal interplay between Lennon and McCartney on the spaced-out "Mother Superior" section; it's a delight.

SIDE TWO

1 Martha My Dear

After all this highly intellectual commentary, we start Side Two with McCartney's paean to his pet sheepdog. And why not? It's quintessential McCartney—melodious, jaunty, and upbeat—and it makes great use of brass and piano arrangements.

What more can we say than the song was later covered by those hobnail-booted—but with no mirrors thereon—fellows, Slade?

2 I'm So Tired

The perfect wee-hours song for insomniacs everywhere contains some acerbic twists of Lennon on lines such as "I'd give you everything I've got for a little peace of mind," and—the great man having apparently smoked one cigarette too many—a righteous "Curse Sir Walter Raleigh." As his lack of sleep raises Lennon's irritation levels, he is backed ably by Harrison's angry lead guitar. Who doesn't sympathize with a sleepless singer?

3 Blackbird

Under the influence of Donovan, this number sees McCartney adopt a wondrous acoustic fingerpicking style—and, influenced by the great British folk guitarists such as Bert Jansch and Davey Graham, producing the remarkable "Blackbird." The song is beautifully melodic and understated, and leaves the listener full of optimism and hope. Who knew that McCartney, "only the bass player," had the ability to dream up such a wonderful composition on guitar?

4 Piggies

Another Harrison-penned song, and one of an increasing number of his tunes deemed worthy in this period to pass through Lennon and McCartney's creative control. It features a fittingly sardonic vocal from The Quiet One, once again addressing matters of class. He rails against the unenlightened middle classes who "with all their backing," he decides, need a "damn good whacking." It has a magnificent harpsichord interlude, too.

5 Rocky Raccoon

We're nothing if not impartial here, and it's genuinely difficult to defend this piece of McCartney-inspired whimsy. Although this slight song—a quirky, tongue-in-cheek western parody—might have been mildly amusing back then, it palls now, and if *The White Album* had been a single record, this track would surely have been dropped. Compare this song to the earlier "Blackbird" and you'll ask yourself how it could possibly have come from the same songwriter.

6 Don't Pass Me By

The obligatory Ringo-sung number is the familiar plea for romantic acceptance—and look, you know what to expect by now. The song pushes no particular sonic boundaries, but that's just fine. The backing track is tinged with an unmistakable country and western flavor—the sound of creative control gone astray, or an example of The Beatles casting their sonic net wide? You can work that one out.

7 Why Don't We Do It in the Road?

This was The Beatles' most upfront song about sex to date, and was—perhaps surprisingly—the fruit of McCartney's imaginings. Propelled neatly along by a driving beat, hand claps, staccato drumming, and piano, we're supplied with the theme of sexual abandon both lyrically and musically. This song is rightly felt to be one of The Beatles' better late-career album tracks, perhaps because it espouses the questioning, no-boundaries ethos of the era so well.

8 I Will

The album's big romantic ballad, "I Will" has a pleasantly throwaway calypso feel, and although it comes nowhere near McCartney's earlier and better efforts at balladry—see the peerless "Blackbird," "Yesterday," and "Here, There and Everywhere"—it's still a charming »

"BLACKBIRD" was a McCartney solo performance. He later revealed the lyrics were inspired by the Civil Rights Movement in America.

ERIC Clapton became good friends with George in the late sixties, and the pair continued to perform together on many post-Beatles projects.

> "I SAID, 'ERIC'S GOING TO PLAY ON THIS ONE,' AND IT WAS GOOD BECAUSE THAT THEN MADE EVERYONE ACT BETTER."
>
> **GEORGE HARRISON**

song. It wouldn't be unfair to consider it an example of the padding that makes *The White Album* a tad flabby in parts, but still, give it a whirl by all means.

9 Julia

The White Album gets serious with "Julia," Lennon's thoughts on the subject of his late mother, who had been killed in a car accident when he was a child. In his later solo career, he revisited the theme in an attempt to purge the trauma—see "My Mummy's Dead" and the heartbreaking "Mother," the latter executed with the assistance of primal scream therapy. Here, Lennon sings this stark, unadorned number accompanied only by an acoustic guitar. It is emotive, naked, and by definition free from any predefined notion of being a Beatle-type song.

SIDE THREE

1 Birthday

What's great about the space afforded to The Beatles by the double-album format is that they can include songs for the fun of it: not every composition has to be weighty and meaningful. This upbeat rocker has a great, raucous vocal from McCartney and might well have been designed—with its "I'm glad it's your birthday" refrain—to be played at parties the world over. You can't help but enjoy this effective Little Richard tribute.

2 Yer Blues

In a similar vein, here The Beatles plan a full-on blues assault, in acknowledgement of the late-sixties British blues boom—think Fleetwood Mac, Chicken Shack, and so on. In true bluesman form, the song comes with a raw vocal from Lennon and self-pitying lyrics—"Yes, I'm lonely," he sings. It's one of the more successful heavy Beatles songs, presaging the kind of heartfelt confessional that Lennon would employ in his solo career.

3 Mother Nature's Son

"Mother Nature's Son"—cut from the same musical cloth as "Blackbird"—has a wonderful, haunting melody at its heart, and is, perhaps, another product of The Beatles' mystical Indian experience. It benefits hugely from the brass overdub at the ending, suggested by the venerable George Martin.

4 Everybody's Got Something to Hide Except Me and My Monkey

This rocker mines a similar vein to "Happiness is a Warm Gun"—certainly in terms of its lyrical imagery. "Monkey" is upbeat throughout, particularly when Lennon exhorts us to "come on," and again on the chorus line. It's a joyous, deliberately retrograde rock 'n' roll romp at the very end of the psych era, making imaginative use of unorthodox instrumentation such as a fire drill in the backing track.

The presence of Yoko Ono in the studio affected the Lennon-McCartney dynamic. Until then, it had been a band policy to avoid bringing wives or girlfriends to the studio.

5 Sexy Sadie

This song is a thinly-veiled attack on The Beatles' former meditative guru, the Maharishi Mahesh Yogi, who had been reported to have betrayed his own teachings to try it on with none other than Mia Farrow. Whether this allegation was true or not—and much doubt has been cast on this story over the years—"Sadie" is possessed with both anger and sarcasm in abundance, driven by the classic rock 'n' roll contrivance of a person wronged.

6 Helter Skelter

Here, The Beatles attempt heavy rock, the gauntlet having been thrown down by Who guitarist Pete Townshend's claim in 1967 that his group was the world's heaviest band, on their most infamous track. They pull it off, too, but unfortunately the song is steeped in rock legend for all the wrong reasons, with its connections to the murderous Charles Manson and his so-called "family" of followers. Get past that, though, and "Helter Skelter" is a blistering aural assault, featuring McCartney's finest rock vocal—particularly on the song's manic chorus. It threatens to end on several occasions, but finally comes to an exhausted halt on the four-minute mark with Ringo's exclamation of "I've got blisters on my fingers!" You know how he feels.

7 Long, Long, Long

Back in calmer waters, "Long, Long, Long" is this side's closer, penned by George Harrison. It's steeped in the kind of mysticism that would later become synonymous with the Dark Horse, and is pervaded with a wistful sense of melancholy. Like all the best songs, it is an all-too-brief treat for the listener that resonates long after the closing chord. One of Harrison's finest compositions.

SIDE FOUR

1 Revolution 1

"Revolution 1," in its *White Album* guise at least, suffers in comparison to the version that backed the contemporaneous "Hey Jude" single. It's far slower, for a start—so much so that the political leanings of Lennon's lyrics, which are a world away from the boy-meets-girl themes of Beatlemania just four years before—are almost lost among the doo-wop backing vocals and relaxed brass adornments. Thank goodness that McCartney deemed it too slow to be a single: otherwise it's doubtful that Lennon would have been provoked into transforming ⏵

1968 was a tumultuous time in the band's personal lives, with relationships ending, others beginning, and each member craving more independence.

"Revolution" into the forceful rocker that we all know and love.

2 Honey Pie

No revolutionary sympathies on display here! On "Honey Pie," The Beatles give way once again to McCartney's fondness for dancehall pastiche. Although the song is immaculately conceived, with interesting sound effects and Lennon doing his best Django Reinhardt impression, the thrills soon dissipate on repeated listens. McCartney's later solo career was full of such self-indulgences, as even his most devoted fans would admit.

3 Savoy Truffle

Now here's a less-than-heavyweight song. The Beatles, minus the absent Lennon, run through Harrison's tale of how his good friend Eric Clapton's penchant for chocolate would inevitably result in frequent trips to the dentist. This amusing tale features a slightly cheesy brass accompaniment, but is nonetheless a pleasant piece of pop. Bon appetit!

4 Cry Baby Cry

"Cry Baby Cry" is, like "Dear Prudence" and so many Beatles classics, both

> ## "I FELT LIKE AN OUTSIDER. BUT THEN I REALIZED THAT WE WERE ALL FEELING LIKE OUTSIDERS."
>
> RINGO STARR

ABOVE Ringo grew frustrated and briefly left the band in August '68. He returned after receiving a telegram from the band saying, "You're the best rock 'n' roll drummer in the world. Come on home, we love you."

ABOVE RIGHT John and Paul went on a press trip to the US to promote the newly formed Apple Corps in May 1968. The band naïvely attempted to manage the company themselves, but their lack of business experience left Apple Corps in disarray.

enjoyable and sinister, more than making up for some of the earlier less-than-essential meanderings on this album. Although Lennon later dismissed it as "a piece of rubbish," it successfully conjures up images of childhood through its use of fairytale characters and nursery rhymes, but beneath such pleasantries it has a distinctly creepy atmosphere that will haunt the listener. What's not to like?

5 Revolution 9

Clocking in at a mammoth 10 minutes, the deeply complex "Revolution 9" is a million miles away from the era of the lovable moptops who expounded harmless ditties such as "Love Me Do." Formed of the extras left over from "Revolution 1," it is a tape-looped extravaganza that rewards the listener with something different each time you hear it. By turns shocking and sinister—see the repeated BBC tones of "number nine"—this song, if you can call it that, remains a dazzling example of The Beatles' avant-garde awareness.

6 Good Night

A gentle lullaby crooned by Ringo Starr, "Good Night" closes *The White Album* on a softer note, soothing the ears after the aural assault of the previous song. In retrospect, *The White Album* is proof that all clichés have some basis in fact—in this case, the maxim that many double albums would have been far better as single records. That said, many of the progressive rock acts that followed The Beatles failed to pay heed to this wisdom, and many of them fared well, so perhaps it's a case of horses for courses. Without a doubt, a number of the ditties here should have stayed as Maharishi-era campfire songs. How else do you explain lapses such as the woeful "Rocky Mountain" and "Honey Pie"? On the other hand, if you sequence all the worthwhile songs—"Happiness Is a Warm Gun," "Dear Prudence," and so on—you'll have a playlist that is among the very finest the world has ever seen.

"WHAT'D WE KNOW ABOUT MAKING MOVIES? ABSOLUTELY NOTHING."

JOHN LENNON

A HARD DAY'S NIGHT 1964

HELP! 1965

MAGICAL MYSTERY TOUR 1967

YELLOW SUBMARINE 1968

LET IT BE 1970

THE SINGLES

Even if you think you know The Beatles' studio albums inside out, have you listened to their non-album singles? You've missed out on a weird and wacky treat—let us guide you through them.

1 From Me to You / Thank You Girl
Released **April 11, 1963**

A-SIDE
From Me to You

"Da da da da da dum dum da," The Beatles informed us at the top of "From Me to You," many fans' gateway drug to The Beatles, and a song which remains fresh to this day. A little brighter than the previous year's single "Love Me Do"—Parlophone must have thrown an extra three farthings at George Martin's studio budget—the song and its all-big-grins sentiments are pleasantly meaningless . . . but then again, so is all the best pop music.

B-SIDE
Thank You Girl

A touch more upbeat than the flipside and definitely more straightforward in its message, "Thank You Girl" is Lennon and McCartney's early attempt to show that they could be nice boys after all, despite the not-entirely-savory message of contemporary songs such as "Please Please Me." As always in this early era, the impact of the tune lies mainly in its repeated chorus hookline, a chance for the chaps to show off their ravishing harmonies.

2 She Loves You / I'll Get You
Released **August 23, 1963**

A-SIDE
She Loves You

An awe-inspiringly great song to this day, "She Loves You" features one of the first of the gorgeous multipart vocal layers for which The Beatles became rightly famed. As the anthem sung by the Liverpool crowd during the vigil for John Lennon's death 17 years later after its

first release—New York's equivalent crowds sang "Give Peace a Chance," tellingly—the song was adopted by millions as the quintessential Fabs composition. Sure, it's a little naïve—but wasn't that the whole point?

B-SIDE
I'll Get You

Look, it might be a little tricky to get past the "Oh yeahs" at the beginning of this slight song. Once past this obstacle, we're into a mildly raucous love song that excels—as was so often the case in the band's early compositions—with the backing vocals. Keep an ear open for a particularly skilful moment in the chorus when McCartney's harmony goes up while Lennon's goes down, always a successful arranging trick.

3 I Want to Hold Your Hand / This Boy
Released **November 29, 1963**

A-SIDE
I Want to Hold Your Hand

Another superlative single, "I Want to Hold Your Hand"—rather like the broadly similar "I Wanna Be Your Man"—is a deceptively simple, energetically youthful expression of amorous juvenilia and not much else—except, of course, that it is delivered in a vehicle that remains completely unforgettable. Where to start with this iconic song? Perhaps with that classic descending chord sequence in the

chorus, and certainly with the amazing way that the singers make the word "hand" extend to seven syllables or more (count them if you don't believe us).

B-SIDE
This Boy

Meanwhile, "This Boy" is a successful fusion of heartstring-twanging pathos and balladry. Slowed down to the point of catatonia and with the lugubrious vocals rendered in the lower register, the song takes off when McCartney

LEFT During The Ed Sullivan Show on February 9, 1964, The Beatles performed "She Loves You" and "I Want to Hold Your Hand" alongside album tracks.

ABOVE The band pictured during the recording of "From Me to You" / "Thank You Girl" at Decca Studios in March 1963.

and Lennon deliver a rousing "Oh, oh-oh-oh, this boy . . . won't be happy . . ." and so on. It complements its A-side very well indeed, in tone, style, and lyric.

4 I Feel Fine / She's a Woman
Released November 23, 1964

A-SIDE
I Feel Fine
Was the opening feedback to this zippy song simply a mistake, or a stroke of Beatle genius? Whatever the case, the catchy central riff and the infectious hook of the chorus equate to an essential slice of feel-good pop. Did you know that on the famous occasion in 1965 when The Beatles met Elvis Presley, the King showed the upstart princes his prowess on the bass guitar by playing the riff to this very song?

B-SIDE
She's a Woman
The self-evidently-titled "She's a Woman" has much to recommend it, not least an astounding Little Richard-esque vocal from McCartney and a wandering bass that sits slickly beneath the guitar stabs that form the structure of the song. When the chorus arrives, the song takes off into airy territory, making it one of the more enjoyable B-sides from a period in The Beatles' career when they were still finding their compositional feet, so to speak.

5 We Can Work It Out / Day Tripper
Released December 3, 1965

A-SIDE
We Can Work It Out
"We Can Work It Out" was a true McCartney and Lennon collaboration, and became the fastest-selling Beatles single since "Can't Buy Me Love." More pensive and restrained than almost any Beatles song to date, it's an elegy towards troubled relationships that resonates to this very day. Your heart will break in the "Life is very short" section.

B-SIDE
Day Tripper
"Day Tripper" stakes a good claim to be an A-side that never was, as a faster, more upbeat, generally "bigger" song than "We Can Work It ▸▸

"All You Need Is Love" debuted on the *Our World* live satellite link up on June 24, 1967. The show was watched by some 400 million people around the world.

Out." The combination works perfectly, though, with "Day Tripper" built on a monumental riff and exuding a certain melancholy vibe. There's a touch of typical Beatles rudeness in the line "She's a prick-teaser," clearly audible in the mix and passed off in public as "She's a big teaser"—but childish as this undoubtedly was, it's a clear sign that The Beatles were ready to push against the establishment.

6 Paperback Writer / Rain
Released May 30, 1966

A-SIDE
Paperback Writer

The focus of The Beatles' eleventh single was a foray into the Swinging London of the young and the hip, with the harmonies on the chorus worth the price of admission alone—and that riff was enough to sell a million Rickenbacker guitars, of course. Listen out for McCartney's frantic octave fills on the bass as each verse begins.

B-SIDE
Rain

"Rain" is a fine lysergic creation, with its revolutionary backward opening lines. In an alternate universe, this song would have been the single A-side—and if it had, we would all no doubt be communicating by telekinesis. This release was an easy number one single by some distance, and it's hard to think of a finer pair of songs ever released on 45.

7 Penny Lane / Strawberry Fields Forever
Released February 13, 1967

A-SIDE
Penny Lane

Has any single matched this double A-side

for sheer invention and perfection? Pink Floyd's "See Emily Play," also released in '67, came mighty close, save for the fact it was one-sided. The hands-down winners must be The Beatles for this high water mark in British single history. This song's brassy evocation of the abnormal among the normal—for example, the very strange fireman in the pouring rain—is the perfect companion to the heartwarming music.

B-SIDE
Strawberry Fields Forever

John Lennon's stunning Mellotron-based recollection of the sacred "Strawberry Fields" of his childhood was light-years ahead of its time. He takes an innocent image of yesteryear and infuses it with psychedelic whimsy, evoking sensations that are never quite everyday—and often a little disturbing.

8 All You Need Is Love / Baby, You're a Rich Man
Released July 7, 1967

A-SIDE
All You Need Is Love

Yes, this song is naïve and reductive, but by this point in their careers, The Beatles could get away with almost anything. With deliberately simple lyrics for an international audience, at best, this song was commercial

counterculturalism, despite the knowingly self-referential "She Loves You" touches on the fade. At worst, it was a call for world peace at a surprisingly low level of sophistication. It's still a classic, though.

B-SIDE
Baby, You're a Rich Man

In contrast, "Baby, You're a Rich Man" on the flip—with its "How does it feel to be one of the beautiful people?" refrain—is stoned immaculate. It's a deliberately slight song, based on a fragile piano and bass backing, and falsetto vocals that seep from the speakers. It's not essential, even if it has a certain playful charm.

9 Hello, Goodbye / I Am the Walrus
Released November 24, 1967

A-SIDE
Hello, Goodbye

Catchy to the point of immortality, this song's extended "Hey la" ending renders "Hello, Goodbye" an effective slice of bubblegum psych pop—and it's worth it for the accompanying visuals (check *YouTube*!) of the quartet playing this tune in their full *Sgt. Pepper* regalia. ➸

The band performing "Hello Goodbye" while filming a TV show at the Saville Theatre in 1968.

B-SIDE
I Am the Walrus

The Walrus was Paul! That was the consensus . . . although who knows what really held true in the dream world conjured up by Lennon in this milestone song? Three parts Lewis Carroll to four parts acid for breakfast, the lyrics place Lennon squarely as the Walrus, as fans of Carroll's 1871 novel *Through The Looking-Glass* will spot. In doing so, he made a strange choice, as that creature represented Victorian capitalism.

10 Lady Madonna / The Inner Light
Released **March 15, 1968**

A-SIDE
Lady Madonna

What a comeback! "Lady Madonna" is the sound of The Beatles bouncing back after the critical pasting they received for *Magical Mystery Tour*. It's essentially a good-time boogie-woogie dance tune, based on a similar groove to that of Humphrey Lyttelton's "Bad Penny Blues." A back-to-basics belter, it enthralled fans of the new, grown-up Fab Four.

B-SIDE
The Inner Light

"The Inner Light" is a lesser-known delight in the catalogue, the product of George Harrison's fascination with transcendental meditation and one of his finest moments in or out of The Beatles. It's a perfect blend of Indian instrumentation and *Sgt. Pepper*-style psych-out.

11 Hey Jude / Revolution
Released **August 26, 1968**

A-SIDE
Hey Jude

Paul McCartney's comforting message to Lennon's son Julian was declared by John to be the best thing that Paul ever wrote. It's hard to disagree with that judgment, as it was among the first—and definitely the best—of rock's obligatory sing-along anthems. It would spawn many copyists in ensuing decades, a tribute to its long-lasting appeal. But what does "the movement you need is on your shoulder" actually mean?

B-SIDE
Revolution

Lennon's rabble-rousing rocker "Revolution" could easily have been a single in its own right, tearing up the nation's record players with its overdriven guitar tones and the great man's sneering thoughts about people who try to solve problems with empty rhetoric. One of the finest-ever anti-protest protest songs.

12 Get Back / Don't Let Me Down (with Billy Preston)
Released **April 11, 1969**

The free-form blues homage of "Get Back" (see *Let It Be* for a deeper analysis on page 114) is balanced nicely by "Don't Let Me Down," a significant composition for its truly impassioned vocal from Lennon and able support from the legendary Billy Preston. Although there are those who never regarded The Beatles as a serious soul act, this superior piece of songwriting tends to suggest otherwise.

ABOVE LEFT Paul was like an uncle to John and Cynthia's young son, Julian. "Hey Jude" was written for him during his parents' divorce in 1968.

ABOVE John and Yoko were married in Gibraltar on March 20, 1969. "The Ballad of John and Yoko" was written on their honeymoon in Paris.

13 The Ballad of John and Yoko / Old Brown Shoe

Released May 30, 1969

A-SIDE
The Ballad of John and Yoko

This unusual A-side diarises, in rather self-pitying tones, the trials and tribulations of the countercultural duo of the day, John Lennon and Yoko Ono. That being said, it remains a pleasingly funny, semi-autobiographical account of the two icons, although its sadly prophetic line of "They're gonna crucify me" may send a shiver down a spine or two.

B-SIDE
Old Brown Shoe

The shuffle beat and sharp lyrical content of "Old Brown Shoe" makes it well worth flipping this single over. Just listen to that powerful beat, the unnerving chord change in the second line of each verse, and those sinister piano and chord fills. The energy of the band at this point is evident, with guitar slides, deft fingerstyle on the bass, and those slightly discordant vocal harmonies making it clear that The Beatles were at the peak of their considerable powers here.

14 Let It Be / You Know My Name (Look Up the Number)

Released March 6, 1970

The overwrought symbolism of this A-side is discussed more deeply in the *Let It Be* section on page 114, but you'll enjoy "You Know My Name (Look Up the Number)" on the flip—it's a comic novelty delivered as only The Beatles can deliver. Bass and piano kick off the song, and an unnervingly chaotic cluster of shouted vocals make it clear that "funny" and "scary" are adjectives that coexist comfortably in The Beatles' world. Spoken words, eerily close-at-hand muttered vocals and the sound of Ringo Starr apparently hitting a trash can lid make up this bizarre composition.

THE band rehearses "All You Need is Love" for the *Our World* event, broadcast live from Abbey Road on June 25, 1967.

ABBEY ROAD STUDIOS

On June 6, 1962, four unknown lads from Liverpool tramped into an elegant Georgian townhouse in North London. As Paul McCartney reflected in a TV interview, Abbey Road Studios—or EMI Recording Studios, as it was then known—didn't roll out the red carpet when the fledgling Beatles arrived to audition for the record label in Studio Two. "I remember the very first day we walked into Abbey Road as four twenty-something boys. We came in the tradesman's entrance, because we weren't allowed to come through the control room, that was for the grown-ups."

In an untouchable hot streak between 1962 and 1969, this was where The Beatles recorded 190 of their 210 songs; rewrote the rulebook of studio production; stretched the possibilities of pop music; fought and reconciled; and smoked, bantered, and hid from the world. For seven years—and more sporadically for the half-century after their 1970 split—Abbey Road was the band's home, playground, and fortress. These four walls were the backdrop to their lives, from the greatest creative triumphs to the most desperate personal lows.

ABBEY ROAD

Released **September 26, 1969**

The Beatles' last stand was perhaps their finest hour. In 1969, John, Paul, George, and Ringo came together, one final time, to produce a classic.

....

SIDE ONE

1 Come Together

With a thinly-veiled Lennon as central protagonist, "Come Together" is a groove-based espousal of the counterculture rich in self-confessed "gobbledygook," that references Yoko Ono (then recovering from a car accident in a hospital bed actually located in Abbey Road Studios) and features the zeitgeist-defining line "you got to be free." All four Beatles featured, with Lennon on double-tracked guitar solo, McCartney bass and piano, and Ringo shuffling beautifully on juju drums. Outwardly good-natured, there was tension in the air. McCartney told Ray Coleman: "On 'Come Together,' I'd have liked to have sung harmony with John, and I think he'd have liked me to, but I was too embarrassed to ask him."

2 Something

George Harrison didn't make many dents in Lennon and McCartney's songwriting predominance, but when he did, he made them count. "Something"—with Harrison taking double-tracked lead vocal and delivering a soaring complementary guitar solo to die for—was his masterpiece. Lennon added piano and a four-minute extended instrumental coda (ultimately shelved but for a small snippet in the middle-eight), while McCartney's over-busy bass vied—perhaps jealously—for attention. With a suggestion of Hammond from Billy Preston, "Something" was released as a double A-side (with "Come Together") as *Abbey Road*'s sole single. Second only to "Yesterday" as the most covered song in The Beatles' catalogue, both Lennon and McCartney have admitted it was the best track on the album. High praise indeed.

3 Maxwell's Silver Hammer

When it comes to bones of contention between Lennon and McCartney,

TOP In an interview, John later commented that he would have done a better job on the vocals for "Oh! Darling" than Paul. "If he had any sense, he should have let me sing it," he joked.

ABOVE McCartney had his first ideas for "Maxwell's Silver Hammer" while the band were at the ashram in Rishikesh.

RIGHT George Harrison's "Something" is one of the most widely covered Beatles tracks, and arguably rivals Lennon and McCartney at their best.

"Maxwell's Silver Hammer" is a veritable skeleton. Outwardly, a jaunty music hall number, its lyric told of medical student Maxwell Edison's predilection for mass murder. Yet while McCartney believed implicitly in his macabre composition's hit potential, driving the band to distraction (with the exception of the absent Lennon, who hated this latest example of what he disparagingly referred to as "Paul's granny music") as he attempted to deliver a definitive version over grueling sessions in July 1969, his fellow Beatles were less than enthusiastic. As successive takes ground on, Harrison told McCartney: "You've taken three days. It's only a song." According to Starr: "It was the worst track we ever had to record."

4 Oh! Darling

McCartney returned to the previous decade for "Oh! Darling." It was a canny combination of traditional rock 'n' roll tropes, blues-rooted, Louisiana swamp pop, and close harmony vocals, ultimately overwhelmed in the final mix by a lead vocal in thrall of Little Richard. McCartney worked hard to nail the right performance, arriving early into Abbey Road, warming his voice up over understated preparatory takes before finally letting rip in pursuit of the kind of raw perfection he'd routinely nail after three hours behind the microphone in Hamburg. John Lennon's piano hammered a complementary Fats Domino accompaniment, but by this stage, the tension was never far from the surface. "'Oh! Darling' was a great one of Paul's that he didn't sing too well," Lennon gleefully highlighted, "I always thought I could have done it better—it was more my style than his." Ouch. Though he might have had a point. Caught on the right night, Lennon was still muscular rock 'n' roll's finest vocal exponent.

5 Octopus's Garden

In August '68, following an argument with Paul over the drum part for "Back in the U.S.S.R.," Ringo temporarily left The Beatles and headed to Sardinia for a family holiday. While ➤➤

"WE DID ACTUALLY PERFORM LIKE MUSICIANS AGAIN."

GEORGE HARRISON

Words: Ian Fortnam. Images: The Beatles (album cover); CBS Photo Archive/Getty Images; (McCartney & Lennon); Keystone-France/Getty Images (Rishikesh); Ed Caraeff/Morgan Media/Getty Images (Harrison)

sailing the Mediterranean on Peter Sellers' yacht, the ship's captain informed him that octopuses collect stones and shells while patrolling the sea bed and construct underwater gardens. Eager to escape the bickering of his bandmates, Starr found solace in songwriting and delivered "Octopus's Garden." It was refined by Starr alongside George Harrison upon his return to Abbey Road during the "Get Back" sessions, and perfected with the entire band reunited and self-producing in July '69. An inoffensive nursery ditty that featured a characteristically lugubrious lead vocal from Starr and undersea sound effects from McCartney—bubbling through a straw into a glass of milk, "Octopus's Garden" has been called, accurately if uncharitably, "a poor man's 'Yellow Submarine.'"

6 I Want You (She's So Heavy)

The first song initiated for *Abbey Road* was one of the last completed; "I Want You (She's So Heavy)" was the longest track the quartet recorded (save for musique concrète sound collage "Revolution 9"). The composition saw John Lennon not so much smitten with Yoko Ono as completely obsessed, and its twelve-word lyric nags undeniably. "I want you, I want you so bad, it's driving me mad," an insistent circular repetition asserts, resignation turns to desperation as riffs echo support, before the awestruck admission "She's so heavy." The track clearly engaged the dissolute band, providing their final hurrah as an airtight ensemble: Harrison bolstering the circular riff's might, McCartney playing out of his skin, and Starr operating a wind machine over the final mesmerizing tumult. With Billy Preston's presence (on Hammond) ensuring a veneer of in-band courtesy, "I Want You" captured latter-period Beatles at their best.

SIDE TWO

1 Here Comes the Sun

In April 1969, George Harrison decided to "sag off" yet another Apple business meeting with "dopey accountants" to spend the day truanting in Eric Clapton's Surrey garden, where Harrison conjured up "Here Comes the Sun" on a borrowed acoustic guitar. The brightly beaming hopeful light to the ultimately oppressive shade of "I Want You," "Here Comes the Sun" represented the relief and optimism Harrison felt when removed from the grind of The Beatles' business machinations and ever more incessant infighting. By the time Harrison brought it into the studio in early July, John Lennon was absent following his aforementioned car crash, so Harrison's bright arpeggiated triads and gently wavering Moog only found McCartney's bass and Starr's drums in support. The song's simplistic positivity proved to be just as infectious as it was tangible, and its popularity has endured—at the date of publication, it is the band's most-streamed track on Spotify.

2 Because

With Lennon, McCartney, and Harrison overlaying three sets of close vocal harmonies in order to achieve a nine-voice choral effect, as Starr gently tapped his hi-hat metronomically, "Because" was the last track that all four Beatles worked on from start to finish. Upon hearing Yoko Ono playing Beethoven's "Piano Sonata No.14 (Moonlight Sonata)," a somewhat chemically enhanced Lennon had her play its chords backwards, and stumbled upon the melody that was to become "Because." The opiated idealistic imagery of its lyric was meanwhile inspired,

just as "Imagine" would be later, by Ono's 1964 conceptual art book *Grapefruit*. The band took 23 takes before nailing the ultimate backing track, with Lennon doubling up guitar lines with harpsichord, McCartney on bass, Harrison on upfront Moog, and producer George Martin adding a suggestion of electric spinet to enhance a prevailing medieval feel. Once the vocals were added, with Studio 2's lights dimmed in a soothing haze of Harrison-provided incense, "Because" sounded more hymn than hit.

3 You Never Give Me Your Money

McCartney was reluctant to give up on The Beatles, but if the end was nigh, he was determined the band should go out on a high. *Abbey Road*'s second side was to climax in an ambitious medley. Superficially, a multipart song cycle appears to be a brave artistic endeavor: a magnum opus; practically speaking, it's an extremely effective method by

JOHN AND YOKO'S T.V. FILM BRILLIANT

EVENING STANDARD

ABOVE "You Never Give Me Your Money" was Paul's thinly veiled objections to Allen Klein's (left) influence and his handling of the band's finances.

BELOW LEFT Paul relaxing at his father's home in July 1968. It was here he was inspired to write "Golden Slumbers."

which to sweep together a bunch of unfinished snippets—some of which had been hanging around since the *White Album* sessions—and rebrand them as your masterpiece. The medley's opening section, McCartney's "You Never Give Me Your Money," is similar in structure to Lennon's "Happiness is a Warm Gun" and composed of five clear constituent parts. From its opening melancholic piano to its concluding "I Want You" echoing guitar arpeggios, "Money" is the Long Medley in microcosm, a linear suite with, at its heart, a resigned McCartney plaintively intoning, "nowhere to go."

4 Sun King

Opening with a sultry reverbed guitar (which George Harrison admitted had been inspired by Fleetwood Mac's

"Albatross") John Lennon's "Sun King" cross-fades up out of Paul McCartney's tacked-on wind-chime and tape-looped conclusion to "You Never Give Me Your Money." Recorded as a single sequential piece with "Mean Mr. Mustard," "Sun King" set five-part multi-tracked Lennon vocals gently adrift atop a languorous sound bed of cymbal splashed Ringo bongos, meanderingly melodic McCartney bass, gently stereo-panning Harrison guitar, and atmospherically inconspicuous George Martin Lowrey organ. "Sun King" intones a quintet of Beach Boys-informed John Lennons, before embarking upon a predictably inexplicable faux Iberian/Italian coda. "*Cuando para mucho, mi amore de felice corazon*," "We just made up . . . Spanish words that sounded vaguely like something," Lennon revealed. ➥

5 Mean Mr. Mustard

Lennon's "Mean Mr. Mustard" is an earworm of significant potency. Harking back to a character-based music-hall jokiness more readily associated with '67's *Sgt. Pepper* era, "Mean Mr. Mustard" jarred the unsuspecting listener out of the comparatively tranquil sonic siesta of "Sun King." The central character, drawn in typically grotesque Lennon lyrics, was "a dirty old man" who "shaves in the dark" and "kept a ten bob note up his nose," loosely based on a miser Lennon discovered in a newspaper report and fleshed out with McCartney during their Rishikesh downtime. A snippet of an idea that, without being co-opted for the Long Medley might have languished on Abbey Road's cutting room floor.

6 Polythene Pam

Lennon's "Polythene Pam" and McCartney's "She Came in Through the Bathroom Window" can claim a tentative grasp on conceptual continuity for the fact they both share origins in the bizarre exploits of Beatle fans. "Polythene Pam" was sparked by memories of Pat Hodgett, an original Beatles aficionado from the band's days at The Cavern Club. "I used to eat polythene all the time," remembered the woman who came to be known as Polythene Pat, "I'd tie it in knots and then eat it. Sometimes I even used to burn it and eat it when it got cold." Perhaps in order to take significant liberties with his subject's reputation, Lennon altered her name to Pam and remodeled her into a "killer diller" plastic fetishist in "jackboots and kilt" who "looks like a man" over vigorously scrubbed 12-string acoustic guitar.

7 She Came in Through the Bathroom Window

Most daily interactions between fans and Fabs were fine—pleasantries were exchanged, autographs signed, boundaries respected—but on one particular occasion, a ladder was acquired from McCartney's garden and one hardcore fan quite literally came in through the bathroom window. McCartney chronicled the incident in song, characterized by its author's ever-inventive walking bass and complementary lead guitar interactions with George Harrison (not to mention Starr spicing up his percussion with enthusiastically applied whip-cracks), "Bathroom Window" provided the Long Medley with one of its more satisfying highlights.

8 Golden Slumbers

The day after Lennon's aforementioned car crash in Scotland, and with the incautious driver in the hospital, McCartney convened with Harrison and Starr to set to work on another pair of conjoined Long Medley segments. As '68 drew to a close, McCartney was visiting his father's house in Cheshire and as he sat at the piano, he noticed sheet music for Elizabethan poet Thomas Dekker's "Golden Slumbers."

"I can't read music and couldn't remember the old tune," he recalled, "So I just started playing my own tune to it." Over a lush orchestral introduction (12 uncredited violins, four violas, four cellos, a double bass, four horns, three trumpets, and two trombones), "Golden Slumbers" opens with an introductory lyric of textbook piano-driven Paul McCartney melancholia, Dekker's contribution arrives, along with Ringo's drums, at the song's title line. Given significant heft by a McCartney vocal that's decidedly unbecoming of a lullaby, but all the better for it.

9 Carry That Weight

After an even more emotional reading of the opening of "Golden Slumbers," "Carry That Weight" announced itself with a spirited gang vocal chorus from all four Beatles, with Ringo in particularly fine and unmistakable voice. We're clearly approaching the Long Medley's crescendo, and an orchestral setting of "You Never Give Me Your Money" explodes into life. Harrison's arpeggiated guitar ushers in a double-tracked McCartney vocal that's beautifully pitched musically and emotionally, prior to a rousing reprise of the "Carry That Weight" chorus. Here's Paul's emphatic final word on The Beatles, with "You Never Give Me Your Money" ringing in their ears. He had Lennon, Harrison, and Starr (who'd all taken a contrary stance to McCartney in all matters financial throughout *Abbey Road*'s creative process) lustily singing "You're gonna carry that weight a long time." Portentous words McCartney had written in recognition of the fact that none of them would ever truly escape the long shadow cast by their years in The Beatles.

10 The End

This appropriately titled concluding section of the Long Medley catches the upward inclination of the final arpeggios of "Carry that Weight" to arrive in a veritable rush of rock 'n' roll positivity, with every last vestige of bad feeling left on the other side of

the studio door. With an "Oh, yeah!" and an "Alright!" the end-of-term air of celebration is tangible. The hard work's over, the hair's down, and all four Beatles (even Ringo, who's drums had never been recorded in stereo before, let alone let loose in their own right) take a solo; the three guitarists butting heads, overlapping, interlocking, mirroring 1969's changing, less formal, post-Beatles musical landscape. And suddenly, "The End" finally reaches *the end*, and emerging from the searing heat of John Lennon's fuzzed solo, Paul McCartney—insistently chop-sticking

away at the piano—prepares to deliver his final lyrical denouement: "And in the end, the love you take, is equal to the love you make," truly a couplet for the ages. The orchestra swells to a glorious sentimental crescendo, George's guitar gently weeps in sympathy, and there's not a dry eye in the house.

11 Her Majesty

Presented, after a 20-second pause, as an untidy after-thought, "Her Majesty" was originally conceived as a buffer between "Mean Mr. Mustard" and "Polythene Pam,"

but ultimately edited out. In essence it's an affectionate observation that while The Queen's "a pretty nice girl . . . she doesn't have a lot to say," knocked out by McCartney before anyone else arrived in the studio on July 2. It had been set aside to be discarded, but was tagged on to the end of the album for safety by cautious second engineer, John Kurlander—for better or for worse, a last-minute reprieve.

BELOW LEFT Paul's experience of a break-in by obsessive fans inspired "She Came in Through the Bathroom Window."

BELOW Hearing Yoko play "Moonlight Sonata" at the piano gave John the idea for "Because."

"ON 'COME TOGETHER' I SAID 'GIVE ME SOMETHING FUNKY AND SET UP A BEAT,' AND THEY ALL JUST JOINED IN."

JOHN LENNON

1962

1963

1964

1965

1966

1967

1968

1969

Images Pictorial Press. Ltd/Alamy (1962); Keystone/Getty Images (1963); Michael Ochs Archives/Getty Images (1964); AA Film Archive/Help/United Artists/Alamy (1965); Roger Viollet Collection/Getty Images (1966); John Pratt/Keystone/Getty Images (1967); Trinity Mirror/Mirrorpix/Alamy (1968); Blueee/Alamy (1969)

LET IT BE

Released **May 8, 1970**

By the time *Let It Be* was released, The Beatles were already history. How does their final, understated work hold up?

SIDE ONE

1 Two of Us

The mostly acoustic composition "Two of Us" is all about Paul McCartney's relationships: firstly his love for Linda Eastman, soon to become the first Mrs. McCartney, and—more uneasily—his slowly degrading musical partnership with John Lennon. The Everly Brothers-style vocal harmonies between the two lead singers help to make the song a fine album opener, even if it lacks the elegant attack of, say, "Taxman" in the pantheon of "great Beatles-album beginners." Note that an early, electric version of this song was created before the band decided to pursue an acoustic direction, in support of the emotional nature of the lyrics.

2 Dig a Pony

Jammed out in a fairly relaxed fashion, "Dig a Pony"—or "I Dig a Pony," as the US version of the LP mistitled it—begins with a false start; you'll hear Ringo Starr shouting "Hold it!" because he was putting out a cigarette at the time. Based on a lumbering waltz-time riff, this song is a strange brew of countercultural messaging, with Lennon intoning, "You can radiate anything you want!" and other invectives. It was dedicated to Yoko Ono, which makes its assemblage of key phrases—itself the key method behind so much of Ono's conceptual art—a logical premise. Is it listenable, though? That depends on your tolerance for obscure artistic endeavors.

3 Across the Universe

The utterly marvelous "Across the Universe" was maligned in certain quarters, mainly due to the unwarranted intrusions of the producer, the late eccentric—and latterly, incarcerated murderer—Phil Spector. However, it should, by virtue of Lennon's beautiful acid imagery, be ordained as a truly genuine last fluttering of English lysergia. One of the great examples of justice being served in popular music came in 2003, when McCartney ordered the release of a remix of this album called *Let It Be . . . Naked*. The new collection stripped away many of the unwanted sonic flourishes that Spector—and The Beatles' then-manager Allen Klein—had insisted upon. In the case of "Across the Universe," the new version removes strings, choirs, and other extraneous fripperies, leaving the song exactly as it was intended to be—a sweet, acoustic rumination on the experience of moving through the ether, eyes and mind opened wide by the hallucinogenic experience.

4 I Me Mine

This George Harrison song—once again, concerned with the nature of the ego and, also again, influenced by his Indian spiritual studies—was reportedly viewed as filler by the rest of The Beatles, which is a reasonable assessment. Unfortunately, "I Me Mine" is something of a dull rocker, and primarily notable only as the last song the band recorded together. Lyrically it does have some strengths,

LEFT The Beatles performed five songs from *Let It Be* at their unannounced rooftop concert on January 30, 1969.

ABOVE In January 1969, the band recorded hundreds of songs, including a range of covers, and tracks that would eventually be used on *Abbey Road, Let It Be,* and their early solo records.

soon to be un-Fab Four. Audiences reacted positively to its piano gospel feel, its deeply religious overtones—conjuring up the notion of the Virgin Mary—and its simple, emotional arrangement. Now, this song is not for everybody: some critics have found it a little mawkish and earnest over the decades, which is true to an extent. However, its sheer presence cannot be denied, a fact that was underlined when Paul McCartney played the song at the climax of the Live Aid concert in 1985— although its impact was undermined slightly when his vocal mic initially failed to work.

to the extent that Harrison titled his 1980 autobiography after it. However, if you're interested in finding out what the sound of The Beatles on autopilot might be, look no further. On this evidence, the group's inevitable demise was probably the best possible outcome.

5 Dig It
One of the few Beatles songs to be credited to all four members, "Dig It" is another product of free-form word association and ad-libbing. The music is a mildly diverting, gospel-like stew, but on this album we're only treated to 51 seconds of it. On the alternate recording of the *Let It Be* album—a Glyn Johns-produced LP of May 1969 called *Get Back*—this song

extends to four minutes. Another version of the song can be seen in the *Let It Be* movie, jammed casually and lasting 30 seconds longer still. So, was it a case of too little songwriting commitment, too many relaxed jam sessions, and too many versions to choose from?

6 Let It Be
The heart of the *Let It Be* album is, of course, in its title track—one of the most accomplished, and beloved, in the whole of the popular music canon. The appeal of this song lies primarily in its message of hope ("there will be an answer") in times of adversity, and that huge outro section, as opposed to any innovative musical leaps forward by the

7 Maggie Mae
After that mighty epic, it seemed that inspiration had temporarily run dry for The Beatles. Take this little song, for example: the fact that "Maggie Mae"—the bawdy tale of a Liverpudlian working girl, and an old warmup tune for the group—was added to the album at all speaks volumes about their creative spark, or lack of it. However, underneath all the coarseness, there is a certain charm, and even the blandest Beatles album-filler is worth your attention, as we've come to learn.

BELOW Already unhappy with being filmed for *Let It Be*, George briefly left the band in January 1969 after disagreements with John and Paul.

> "WE NEVER HAD MUCH PRIVACY—AND NOW THEY WERE FILMING US REHEARSING . . . IT WAS A VERY, VERY DIFFICULT, STRESSFUL TIME."
>
> GEORGE HARRISON

SIDE TWO

1 I've Got a Feeling

On "I've Got a Feeling"—augmented by Apple signing Billy Preston on piano— The Beatles up the collaborative quotient on this blues-plus-soul fusion of two separate Lennon and McCartney compositions. Shades of "A Day in the Life" on *Sgt. Pepper*, perhaps? Not quite—the song never really elevates itself above mid-table Beatles—but there is some excellent emoting on the song by Lennon, whose contribution was originally titled "Everyone Had a Hard Year." The sentiment certainly held true of the man himself, who had spent 1969 battling a heroin addiction, while his relationship with his son Julian had become rocky and he had endured a sticky divorce from his first wife, Cynthia. That's plenty of songwriting inspiration, right there: sadly, the results weren't all they could have been.

2 One After 909

This pleasant skiffle retread, possibly dating back as far back as 1957, would have been a nostalgic blast for The Beatles to play, but it's a questionable experience for any listener who isn't a devotee of the old Lonnie Donegan style. However, the version we hear on the *Let It Be* album is a live cut, taken from The Beatles' final rooftop performance, helped out again by organist Billy Preston. A cleaned-up version also appeared on *Let It Be . . . Naked*.

3 The Long and Winding Road

Whatever the arguments about the standard of musicality in this song— Lennon's unreliable bass part was said to be a deliberate attempt to sabotage McCartney's composition—the poignancy of the lyrics take on a greater significance when viewed as the soundtrack to the end of The Beatles' wondrous career. The Welsh singer Tom Jones was offered this song by McCartney, but turned it down, only to see it become a huge hit at the hands of Ray Charles in 1973. "Maybe if he'd offered me 'Let It Be' I'd have said yes," quipped Jones some years later.

4 For You Blue

A love song written by George Harrison for his wife Pattie Boyd, "For You Blue" may not be quite in the same league as his majestic "Something," but it definitely retains a certain sweetness. It's a 12-bar country song, essentially, and features Lennon's slick lap-steel guitar performance—who knew he could play C&W so well? It emerged later than Harrison had written the song while hanging out with Bob Dylan in the relaxed environs of New York State, far from the tensions that were so prevalent back home with the band—which explains its happy, optimistic feel.

5 Get Back

Yes, jammed songs really can work—just look at "Get Back," for example, which is a real return to musical authenticity after so many previous psychedelic excesses. The lyrics are free associated, and the song's punchy R&B groove makes for a catchy, worthwhile end to the album. Note that this version differs from the single in several ways: there's some inconsequential studio chat between the musicians, and the reverb is absent on the LP version.

So where does this leave *Let It Be*? Well, in comparison to The Beatles' earlier albums, it suffers from a slightly lazy "let's jam it in the studio and hope for the best" approach. This can and does work, as in "Get Back," for instance, where the results are impressive, but far too often the jams descend into a workmanlike blues—see "I've Got a Feeling" and "Dig a Pony." As we have previously mentioned, parts of the album are drenched in the "celestial strings" production of Phil Spector, which detract somewhat from the bright spots—the beautiful "The Long and Winding Road" and the last puff of psychedelic imagery on "Across the Universe." The end result is a little patchy, but at least there's the all-time genius stroke of "Let It Be" itself to make the album a worthwhile artifact.

BACK TO THE BEATLES' ROOTS

By 1969 the Beatles were in discord. They were still being civil to each other, and some excellent songs were created as the decade came to a close, but internal strife slowly built and each member had his own, individual priorities to deal with. Hampered by creative dissent and disagreeing about management, The Beatles recorded their final work as the *Let It Be* album and film, with their internal tensions both audible and visible.

However, while the band were indeed drifting apart, the fractious portrayal in the *Let It Be* film did not necessarily tell the whole story. This period has also been documented in *The Beatles: Get Back*, a three-part series directed by Peter Jackson, released in November 2021. It has since won a slew of awards, including five Emmy Awards in 2022. The series was made in cooperation with McCartney and Starr, as well as Harrison and Lennon's widows, Olivia Harrison and Yoko Ono.

Speaking about the project, Starr explained: "There was hours and hours of us just laughing and playing music . . . There was a lot of joy and I think Peter will show that."

Jackson was reportedly given 55 hours of original footage to use, including the final rooftop concert from January 30, 1969, but the final cut has been whittled down to just six hours. Settle in for a Beatles binge!

The episodes of *The Beatles: Get Back* are streaming on Disney+.

END OF THE ROAD

"THE Beatles had gone through so much and for such a long time," reflected producer George Martin in *Anthology*.

THE END OF AN ERA

When The Beatles finally called it a day, this seismic event occurred in several stages. You could arguably point to the disarray of the *Let It Be* sessions in early 1969 as the start of their split, or the points before Paul McCartney's official departure on April 10, 1970, when individual members released their first solo albums. The actual split was mired in legal processes, of course, with certain agreements only being finalized in the eighties.

Either way, by 1971 The Beatles were legally history, not that this fact stopped journalists asking them for years when they planned to get back together. As each member devoted the seventies to solo work and extracurricular activities, it became clear that none of them would equal the former band's commercial impact—with the possible exception of McCartney, whose band Wings was selling out stadiums by the end of that decade. However, as we now know, a full reunion was never to occur.

WHAT THE BEATLES DID NEXT

It's been over 50 years since The Beatles called it
a day—and it's been half a century of creativity,
tragedy, and sheer chaos.

....

What happens when the biggest rock band in the world comes apart at the seams? In the case of The Beatles in 1970—all still young, aged just 27 to 29—the race was on to kick-start solo careers without losing momentum. That sounds perfectly doable . . . right?

Well, yes and no. 1970 was Year Zero for the post-Beatles era, even though the band wasn't technically quite over yet. Indeed, some of their outstanding legal and financial disputes weren't resolved until the eighties, and those are just the ones we know about. Still, in 1970 John Lennon, Paul McCartney, George Harrison, and Ringo Starr—listed in order of "Beatle Most Likely to Make It as a Solo Artist"—all released ➤➤

Words: Joel McIver. Images: Ron Howard/Redferns/Getty Images (Lennon); Michael Putland/Getty Images (McCartney; Starr; Harrison)

LEFT John and Yoko formed the Plastic Ono Band for their various projects. Lennon's "Imagine" is arguably his most famous work.

ABOVE Paul enjoyed post-Beatles success with Wings. "Mull of Kintyre" became the UK's best-selling single of all time.

TOP RIGHT George performing with Bob Dylan at The Concert for Bangladesh benefit event he organized with Ravi Shankar.

BELOW RIGHT Ringo with Peter Sellers in 1969's *The Magic Christian*. He continued acting after the band split.

solo albums. How did the music stand up, compared to the golden era of creativity which they'd just left behind?

Lennon's solo work was the most successful at first, with his prolific 1970-75 run of albums packed with thoughtful, if sometimes bitter, songs. However, the albums that he recorded with his wife Yoko Ono demanded a lot of the public, even in the anything-goes seventies: he had already released three albums with her during The Beatles' reign—*Two Virgins* (1968), *Life With the Lions*, (1969) and *The Wedding Album* (also '69). Avant-garde in nature and confrontational in theme, many of his Ono-partnered songs invited ridicule and worse, indifference. In the second half of the seventies, Lennon retreated from the public eye to raise his son, Sean Ono Lennon, only planning a comeback at the end of the decade.

McCartney was prolific too, and like Lennon he recorded with his wife, Linda, but his focus was more ambitious. After his self-titled album and *Ram* received moderate acclaim in 1970-72, he formed a band, Wings, and planned a campaign from grassroots level. At first, Wings toured the UK, doing small university shows to gauge interest. When these proved critically and financially successful, McCartney worked his way up over the remainder of the decade to genuinely phenomenal success, to the point where Wings sold out American stadiums and enjoyed a whole catalogue of hits.

If you're interested in exploring the Wings catalogue, be warned that it's a rather unusual collection of material. Their most commercially successful records—*Band on the Run* (1973), *Venus and Mars* (1975), and *Wings at the Speed*

> "WE CAN GAIN EXPERIENCE FROM THE PAST, BUT WE CAN'T RELIVE IT; AND WE CAN HOPE FOR THE FUTURE, BUT WE DON'T KNOW IF THERE IS ONE."
> **GEORGE HARRISON**

of Sound (1976)—do contain their fair share of greatness, but there's an awful lot of pleasant, self-indulgent twaddle in there too. McCartney's critics, of which there are many, have always pointed to his mindset as a millionaire family man as being detrimental to his art, and there's something to this. How much gripping music can you produce when you're deeply contented with your world, after all?

Jumping back to the early seventies, great things were expected of George Harrison, whose songs in The Beatles—relatively few in number though they were—had often been among the band's very best. His early albums *Wonderwall Music* (1968) and *Electronic Sound* (1969) had their charms, but he really came into his own with the phenomenal triple album *All Things Must Pass* in 1970. Whether he ever equaled that triumph with his later releases—and he too was very productive, issuing albums on a regular basis—is debatable. Where Harrison really excelled was with his charity concerts, organizing The Concert for Bangladesh in New York City in August 1971,

and with one-off pop singles in the eighties. Something of an unexplored talent, perhaps?

As for Ringo Starr—although he scored highly with 1973's eponymous album, which featured the three other former Beatles, the rest of his solo releases have not, shall we say, set the world alight. In fairness, he did enjoy a career in business and as an occasional actor, as well as dealing with—and ultimately defeating—a series of addictions, so he had a lot on his plate. When Starr's albums were successful, as they have occasionally been in critical if not commercial terms, it has usually been because of the caliber of the special guests with which he has collaborated.

Throughout the seventies, the truth is that all four former Beatles labored under the long shadow cast by their old band. With interviewers incessantly asking about a potential reunion, and the successful double albums *Greatest Hits 1962–1966* and *1967–1970*, released in 1973, taking up the public's attention, it was always

going to be difficult for them to establish a solo foothold. The bigger picture, with hindsight, is that as the punk wars raged at the end of the decade, McCartney and Wings were a commercial, if unchallenging, hit; Lennon was a rarely seen, avant-garde maverick; and Harrison and Starr were regarded with affection as once-great, now-fading stars.

All this changed on December 8, 1980, when the most pivotal event of The Beatles' post-sixties careers took place—the murder of John Lennon. Just 40 years old and in the middle of what looked like a reasonably successful comeback with his *Double Fantasy* album, Lennon was shot dead in the Dakota Building, the New York apartment block where he and his family lived.

We all know the facts of what happened next—the return of his song "Imagine" to the top of the charts, the fans' vigils, the refocus on his life and times, the rise of a profitable Lennon-related nostalgia industry. The wider perspective that we can draw here, four decades and counting after the fact, is that his death reframed the entire Beatles concept in the public's eyes: now that they could no longer fully reform, they represented a past that was now lost, suffused with rose-tinted vibes of peace and love. Nothing that McCartney, Harrison, or Starr ever did after this point could be the same as it had been before.

The eighties looked and sounded different without Lennon's acerbic wit, at least in The

Beatles' world. McCartney wound Wings up and turned his focus to a long string of solo records, while Harrison and Starr continued to be loved rather than respected. Their music began to include rearward-looking nostalgia in its themes, with McCartney heading up 1985's Live Aid concert with a set of oldies, and Harrison recording a self-explanatory song called "When We Was Fab" two years later.

Although the eighties had its sartorial and creative downsides for the surviving Beatles, with all three men rocking the mullets and synths of the day with enthusiasm, one upside was the arrival of digital technology. The first CD reissues of The Beatles' catalogue came fairly late, in 1987, with the importance of this move being that the canon was now standardized—as 12 studio albums, the American version of *Magical Mystery Tour,* and a *Past Masters* double album which collected all the non-album material. EMI deleted all other compilations except the two *Greatest Hits* albums: two significant consequences of this decision were that a lot of old Beatles vinyl became highly collectible, and that the path was now clear for a sequence of new compilations—which continues, profitably for everyone concerned, to this day.

In the nineties, the decade of Beatles-indebted Britpop, the band's stock rose even higher. Something about their golden,

10-year reign through the increasingly far-off sixties was attractive to the public as the millennium approached, and—already members of the resolutely backward-looking Rock and Roll Hall of Fame since 1988—the "Threetles" took full advantage. A new live album, *Live at the BBC,* came out in 1994, and the following year McCartney, Harrison, and Starr worked on the massive *Beatles Anthology* project. This encompassed the release of unissued recordings, a TV series, a huge book, three two-CD or three-LP box sets, an eight-volume video collection, and most importantly, two new Beatles songs.

These cuts, "Free as a Bird" and "Real Love" were objects of immediate curiosity and performed spectacularly well. Based on old demos, with Lennon's muffled vocals brought up to modern standards through the miracle of studio technology, the songs were best described as "very Beatley," with the expected descending chords and psychedelic elements. There was a certain macabre charm to Lennon's beyond-the-grave vocals, and the public lined up to enjoy the *Anthology* products, with an estimated 400 million people watching the TV series. Not bad for an "old sixties band."

The vault was mined even further in ➡

Liverpool Echo

No. 31.321   TUESDAY, DECEMBER 9, 1989   10p

Binns
TOY DEPARTMENT
SUPER INTERNATIONAL
TYPEWRITER FROM PETITE.
Usually £16.95.   Now for only **£13.25**

Crazed gunman charged

RUSH   NEW YORK, MONDAY — FORMER BEATLE JOHN LENNON WAS SHOT AND KILLED
TONIGHT AT HIS HOME IN NEW YORK CITY, POLICE SAID.
REUTER 0655

● How the news was broken to the world.

JOHN LENNON SHOT DEAD

JOHN LENNON, of the legendary Liverpool pop group, The Beatles, was shot dead in New York to-day by a crazed gunman.

After a man police described as "a local screwball" pumped five bullets into Lennon, he yelled "I'm shot" and staggered up a few steps into the apartment building where he lived.

And as the 40-years-old superstar lay dying in the arms of his wife, Yoko Ono, his last whispered words were " Help Me," according to neighbour Carrie Rouse.

WORLD HAS LOST A GREAT GUY, SAYS SAD PAUL

The surviving member of Britain's most famous contemporary song-writing team was visibly upset by the news of his former partner's death to-day.

Paul McCartney, who now has his own group, Wings, said: "I can't take it in at the moment," as he drove away from his Sussex cottage in a red Mercedes.

> ## "IF WE CANNOT LOVE OURSELVES, WE CANNOT FULLY OPEN TO OUR ABILITY TO LOVE OTHERS OR OUR POTENTIAL TO CREATE."
>
> **JOHN LENNON**

TOP LEFT Fans gather at the *Strawberry Fields* memorial in New York's Central Park to commemorate various Beatles anniversaries.

ABOVE Dhani and Olivia Harrison organized the Concert for George memorial in 2002 on the anniversary of his death.

1999, when an expanded soundtrack to *Yellow Submarine* was released, and again in 2000 with the appearance of *1*, a collection of Beatles chart-toppers. Bizarrely from our point of view in the Spotify era, *1* became the fastest-selling album of all time, itself hitting number one in 28 countries and selling 31 million copies over the next two decades.

Perhaps the relentless digging into the old catalogue was timely, in retrospect, because the clock was ticking for The Beatles. George Harrison died of lung cancer in November 2001, at only 58 a couple of decades before his time. He'd had a rough couple of years, battling his disease and barely surviving an attack by a violent burglar at his Henley home, and the public was rightly saddened by his early departure. McCartney and Starr joined other musicians at the Concert for George at the Royal Albert Hall in London the following year.

And then there were two.

Anyone expecting Beatles-related activities to diminish, now that only the band's rhythm section remained, will have been taken aback by McCartney and Starr's busy last decade or two. Both men, now knights of the realm, have continued to record and tour, collaborating with each other from time to time, and showing no sign of slowing down.

The wider Beatles industry continues to flourish, too. In 2003, *Let It Be . . . Naked* was released, something of a personal coup for McCartney. The original *Let It Be* album from 1970 was, as you will recall, smothered in orchestral and choral elements against his wishes, the work of the diabolical duo Phil Spector and Allen Klein. With the songs stripped of these cheesy flourishes and released as clean versions, the album re-established its place in the canon and was widely appreciated by fans.

Not everything the two Sirs and their teams do is a solid-gold success; witness the 2009 *Beatles: Rock Band* video game, for example. However, a CD reissue program the same year of The Beatles albums, remastered in stereo, complemented the songs' reappearance in FLAC and MP3 format on a limited edition USB flash drive.

It took a long time for the Fab Four's music to appear on streaming services; as you can imagine, the legal processes that govern the most influential—and let us not forget, most lucrative—collection of music in history must be labyrinthine. Still, iTunes had the music by 2010 and Spotify by 2015, rendering future physical releases less essential than they had previously been.

What is most important, as the remaining two musicians enter their final years of productivity, is that something of the original band's ethos remains. The swell of public affection when McCartney and Starr performed together at the Grammy Awards in 2014 confirmed this. A coinciding TV special, *The Night That Changed America: A Grammy Salute to The Beatles*, reminded the kids who they were watching, and a 2016 movie called *The Beatles: Eight Days a Week* performed a similar function. An even bigger production directed by Peter Jackson called *The Beatles: Get Back* is available for streaming on Disney+.

After all these years, reissues and box sets of The Beatles' albums continue to break sales and chart records. It's one thing when a lot of people love your music; it's quite another when those people actually dig into their pockets to buy that music—and in commercial terms, The Beatles have never been more of a force than they are now. Why is this? McCartney and Starr's new music is decent, but it's hardly *Sgt. Pepper*, after all.

The truth is that The Beatles are now no longer a band, or even a brand. They are a way of life, a whole philosophical approach to existence, encapsulated in those golden songs and illustrated in their followers' minds with images of excitement, rebellion, innocence, and serenity which may not even have existed. Whether they did or not doesn't matter; they will always be loved.

"Now and Then": The Last Beatles Song

On November 2, 2023, the world heard what we all thought impossible: a new Beatles song. Originally written and recorded by John Lennon in 1977 but abandoned unfinished, the psychedelic soft rock ballad was once considered for a Beatles reunion single for *The Beatles Anthology* after John's death in 1980, but was ultimately shelved due to the lack of necessary technology needed to isolate John's vocals. Three decades later, Paul McCartney and Ringo Starr, using machine-learning audio-restoration technology, were able to isolate Lennon's voice from the 1977 demo, add George Harrison's guitar tracks, and produce a crystal-clear song, almost as if the Fab Four had just recorded it in the same room together the other day. Peter Jackson was able to use the same technology for the 2021 documentary *The Beatles: Get Back*, and directed the music video—yes, music video—for the last Beatles song, and final farewell.

RINGO and Paul at the premiere of *The Beatles: Eight Days a Week—The Touring Years* in September 2016.

John and George
pictured together while
filming *Magical Mystery
Tour* in 1967.

A FAREWELL TO HEROES

The murder of John Lennon on December 8, 1980, is the single most shocking homicide in the history of popular music. Shot in the back by a fan, Mark Chapman, at the Dakota Building in New York where he lived with his family, Lennon was pronounced dead in the hospital: the ensuing announcement caused a worldwide wave of grief. Beatles fans in Liverpool and New York staged vigils in tribute; Lennon's solo work began to sell in great numbers; and Chapman remains incarcerated over 40 years later—partly because the authorities at his New York prison have been warned by vengeful Beatles fans that the day Chapman leaves prison will be his last.

Harrison died a less violent but still tragic death, succumbing to cancer in 2001 at the age of only 58. Much loved for his accomplished musicianship, his wide-ranging spiritual explorations and his quiet demeanor in contrast to the bigger personalities in The Beatles, Harrison leaves a considerable legacy. May both creative masters rest in peace.

THE *STRAWBERRY FIELDS* MEMORIAL, NEW YORK

THE *GEORGE HARRISON* MEMORIAL GARDEN, BHAKTIVEDANTA MANOR, UK

The Beatles Statue on Liverpool Waterfront was donated by The Cavern Club and placed in 2015, on the 50th anniversary of the band's last Liverpool gig.

THE LEGACY OF THE BEATLES

If you think The Beatles simply wrote some good songs and flashed a few peace signs, you have more to learn.

....

When The Beatles walked away from each other over 50 years ago, they may—or may not—have realized that they weren't just splitting up a rock band. In effect, they were ending the first stage of a cultural, anthropological, and political revolution that affected almost all sectors of popular life in the sixties, arguably the most dynamic decade in living memory.

Why only the "first stage" of this revolution? Surely The Beatles' influence on our lives ended when the band did? Well, no—the changes they wrought in their decade as a working unit continue to resonate today, half a century later. No other musical entity can make such a claim. Let's see how this came to pass. ➤➤

"WE'RE ALL REALLY THE SAME PERSON. WE'RE JUST FOUR PARTS OF THE ONE."

PAUL McCARTNEY

THE NUMBERS

Let's start by acknowledging the sheer scale of The Beatles' success. Over the sixties, despite that decade's plethora of huge-selling bands and artists, this little beat combo from the unloved seaport of Liverpool dominated the UK, Europe, and North America. Their 1963 single "From Me to You" was the first of a four-year, 11-single run of releases that hit the top of the *Record Retailer* charts, then the primary sales metric in the UK.

In America, meanwhile, as early in their career as April 4, 1964, The Beatles simultaneously occupied the top five chart slots with "Can't Buy Me Love," "Twist and Shout," "She Loves You," "I Want to Hold Your Hand," and "Please Please Me." If that wasn't enough, they also held 11 other positions on the Billboard Hot 100. It was the same story in Australia and Canada, too, where the band held the top six and top nine spots in the charts respectively.

Even in the age of Adele, Drake, Ed Sheeran, and the rest of the chart-dominating mega-sellers, no one has sold as many physical units as The Beatles, who are thought to have shifted 600 million recordings. They also have the record for the most Number 1 albums on the UK Albums Chart, the most Number 1 hits on the Billboard Hot 100 chart, and the most singles sold in the UK.

THE GEOGRAPHY

Now, the big numbers are useful but they don't come close to telling the full story. Before The Beatles conquered America, they stirred up some profound changes in attitude. Before Beatlemania, popular music was entrenched firmly in London, like so many other industries. However, in 1963, the newspapers started using terms like "Merseybeat" and "the Mersey sound"—and suddenly our attention shifted northwards. It's been reported that the rise of Beatlemania even made Scouse a cool, desirable accent in the early sixties, with impressionable youths from Cornwall and Yorkshire trying to sound as if they came from the Wirral.

Think about what that means. Would we ever have heard a regional accent on the BBC all these years later if Lennon and McCartney hadn't demanded people's

LEFT They may not look like rebels, but The Beatles bucked many social conventions of the sixties.

ABOVE Beatlemania: Police officers struggle to hold back screaming fans outside Buckingham Palace as the band receives their MBEs in October 1965.

attention, up there in Merseyside? Would there ever have been a "Sheffield scene" in 1983 or a "Madchester" in 1989 or a "'Cool Cymru" rock movement in 1999 without this precedent?

THE DEMOGRAPHICS

We'll be the first to admit that The Beatles came along at a point when the world was ready for a band like them—they fulfilled a particular need, and fulfilled it perfectly. In the UK and USA, a new breed of music consumer—the teenager—was now being taken seriously by corporate interests. Why? Because, of course, they had money to spend. Economic strictures in the West

after World War II were starting to relax a little, and households were doing better financially, which meant that the kids had pocket money that they could spend—with almost no persuasion required—on hot young guitar slingers who looked cool and rebellious.

And make no mistake, The Beatles looked like rebels, albeit smartly dressed ones. They were working-class—no public school or Ivy League educations for them—which gave them a dangerous edge. These blokes weren't like Frank Sinatra, Perry Como, or Elvis Presley: they were handsome badasses with razor-sharp wit who would either serenade you or humiliate you, depending on their mood. ➡

Images Michael Ochs Archives/Getty Images (press conference, rooftop); Martin Wahlborg/Getty Images (vinyl); Hulton-Deutsch Collection/CORBIS/Corbis/Getty Images (crowd);

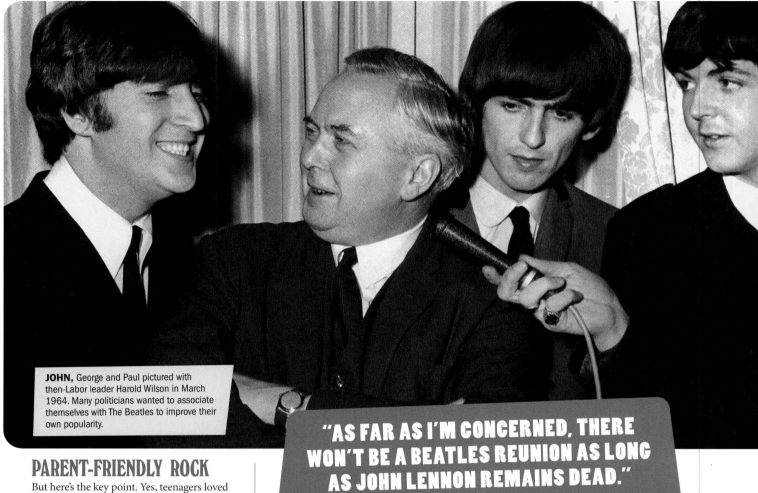

JOHN, George and Paul pictured with then-Labor leader Harold Wilson in March 1964. Many politicians wanted to associate themselves with The Beatles to improve their own popularity.

PARENT-FRIENDLY ROCK

But here's the key point. Yes, teenagers loved The Beatles and their shockingly long hair and withering mockery—but so did their moms and dads, and worse, so did the establishment. In the UK at least, a decline in political conservatism was underway, with National Service abolished and teenage boys free to go out and dance all night rather than polish army boots. Then-Prime Minister Harold Wilson got fully on board with the Fab Four message, wanting to appeal to teens and nab their votes.

As ever, money was at the heart of all this: The Beatles' massive overseas success had generated an export market for British pop music for the first time, assisting the government's balance of payments deficit. No wonder Number 10 was down with Lennon and McCartney, pioneering an uneasy alliance of politicians and rock stars that continues in a rather suspect manner to this day. In the run-up to the 1964 general election, both the major parties referred to The Beatles in speeches in an effort to seem in touch with the people. Of course, nobody bought this ruse, and it soon led to accusations between Labor and the Tories of bandwagon-jumping. It was all pretty undignified.

> **"AS FAR AS I'M CONCERNED, THERE WON'T BE A BEATLES REUNION AS LONG AS JOHN LENNON REMAINS DEAD."**
>
> **GEORGE HARRISON**

The final indicator that the establishment had bought fully into The Beatles came when the band was invited to play the Royal Variety Performance on November 4, 1963. They couldn't very well say no, in the first year of their success, and indeed it was a wise move in commercial terms because the show was watched by a TV audience of 26 million, literally half the population of the UK at the time. Perhaps to show that The Beatles still had teeth despite this ultimate acquiescence to authority, Lennon made his famous mild quip about rattling jewelry, a nicely gauged gag that made him look a bit rebellious but wasn't so cheeky that it got him banged up for treason.

In fact, he and his band received MBEs two years later, after a campaign in *Melody Maker* and the involvement of PM Wilson. Since then, it's been common practice for successful rockers to be bestowed with gongs and even knighthoods, as was later the case with McCartney and Starr, both Sirs these days.

COOL BRITANNIA

It's interesting to note that The Beatles—the first and biggest of the new British Invasion of pop bands looking to infiltrate America—began writing their own material a couple of years into their careers, refusing to cover any more American standards and pioneering the concept of a band that wrote and performed its own music. In other words, they were a cultural unit that people had to take seriously.

In America, the assassination of President Kennedy in November 1963 occurred just 11 weeks before The Beatles played their first live US TV performance on *The Ed Sullivan Show*. Maybe it's a stretch to make this claim so long after the fact, but it's been theorized that the general mood of the country after the shock of such a profound loss meant that the American public was ready, even desperate, for a vivid, forward-looking band such as The Beatles, whose rendition

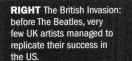

of "I Want to Hold Your Hand" was utterly seismic.

Beatles historian Ian McDonald once said, "Every American artist, black or white, asked about 'I Want to Hold Your Hand' has said much the same: it altered everything, ushering in a new era and changing their lives." It would seem that a large proportion of the *The Ed Sullivan Show* viewers—73 million of them, or about one-third of the entire US population—agreed with this, as a huge number of them promptly formed bands of their own.

Life magazine wrote: "In 1777 England lost her American colonies. Last week The Beatles took them back." The floodgates duly opened, and by the end of '64 a ton of other British bands were doing well in America. Of these, only The Rolling Stones went on to become serious rivals to the Fab Four, but groups such as The Dave Clark Five and Gerry & The Pacemakers did good business too.

It wasn't just America that took the bait, either. According to the *Daily Express*, by 1965 there was a Beatles-like band called The Candid Lads playing in the Soviet Union. Los Shakers, a Uruguayan band heavily influenced by and modeled on the Fab Four, found fame across Latin America. Japan, too, produced its own crop of rock bands who wrote their own stuff. Where would it all end? Perhaps it never has. ➠

ABOVE The band spent several weeks in Rishikesh, India studying meditation under guru Maharishi Mahesh Yogi in March 1968.

BELOW left Beatles fans from all over the world visit Abbey Road Studios to write messages on the wall outside.

BELOW right "I owe a lot of what I do to Little Richard and his style; and he knew it," reflected McCartney. "He would say, 'I taught Paul everything he knows.' I had to admit he was right."

THE IMAGE

The Beatles' aesthetic has always been massively influential. In the early days they wore leathers; later they wore suits; and finally—think of the *Abbey Road* sleeve—they found their individual styles. In every incarnation, they looked supremely cool, probably because the group didn't last as long as the eighties, when fashion fell into a black hole of terribleness. (On a related note, it also helped that no Beatle ever got fat or went bald: there's some good genes there. Look at McCartney and Starr nowadays—both look 20 years younger than their calendar ages.)

The most impactful Beatles era, sartorially speaking, is probably the mop-top haircuts, Pierre Cardin suits, and Cuban heels period that lasted until 1964 or thereabouts. Achingly cool from today's perspective, this look helped to boost the international profile of British fashion—and the associated arts traditions—to the point where Swinging London was a very real phenomenon.

Consider also the group's perfect, if probably inadvertent, combination of traditionally masculine and feminine elements in their look and sound. They pioneered headbanging before the concept was even thought of, in particular McCartney and Harrison, who did a kind of weird-looking head shaking that was the direct precursor to today's common heavy metal technique. At the same time, though, they hinted towards femininity with those long, styled haircuts, and of course their

falsetto vocals. This didn't freak out the more traditional men who saw them on TV because they wore those smart, almost conservative suits.

It's not going too far to pinpoint Beatlemania as the starting point for the free experimentation with gender tropes that has typified the most exciting rock music in subsequent decades. Full credit must go to The Beatles' precursor Little Richard for blazing that trail, but you can draw a direct line from him through The Beatles to David Bowie, Marc Bolan, Freddie Mercury, Boy George, the New Romantics, Peaches, and Lady Gaga.

GROWING UP IN PUBLIC

The Beatles were a band—a serious one, blessed with plenty of creative capital—but this wasn't easy to understand when they were still

head shaking, grinning lads in suits. Behind the early smiles and jokes, the substance of the group was much more profound than their image would suggest, something we expect from our rock bands these days, but which was a novelty back then. They didn't help themselves with their lightweight self-portrayals in the *A Hard Day's Night* and *Help!* movies, of course, or indeed the cartoon series *The Beatles*, which ran from 1965 to 1969 in America.

By 1966 The Beatles were sick of their cheesy teenybopper image, and—coupled with the boredom and fan adulation of their long tours—shed their youthful image and quit the road. Both decisions enabled them to knuckle down to the best work of their lives: the golden sequence of albums from *Revolver* to *Let It Be*. They grew moustaches; they stopped grinning at the camera in photoshoots; and they declined to take part

"I BELIEVE IN EVERYTHING UNTIL IT'S DISPROVED . . . IT ALL EXISTS, EVEN IF IT'S IN YOUR MIND."

JOHN LENNON

in frivolous projects such as the 1967 movie *The Jungle Book*, which had planned a scene of animals singing with Scouse accents.

This was a period of evolution for The Beatles that matters to us today because we expect our musicians to take their job seriously. Moreover, we expect rock and pop music to be capable of functioning as the highest of high art, political commentary, and activist propaganda; this was not a widely held expectation before this band of pioneers made it the norm. If you're a fan of long, complex, multifaceted songs like Queen's "Bohemian Rhapsody" or Radiohead's "Paranoid Android," you know where the license to make such music came from.

As The Beatles grew, so did the significance of their actions. When they spoke out against racial segregation in Florida in 1964, and refused to play a segregated venue, their actions resonated worldwide. When they espoused flower power, the expansion of the mind

through hallucinogens, and an exploration of spirituality through Eastern religious thought, these practices gained legitimacy and therefore traction. They were so much more than just a bunch of musicians: they kick-started real, quantifiable change.

So how do we draw a line under the career of this most influential of bands?

The Beatles changed everything, and that change is their legacy. They made people understand that pop music can be artistic, and it can be political, and it can be ambitious. They saw the world changing around them, and they rode that wave of evolution, writing music that connected with people just as it challenged them. What they did in that sense is totally relevant today.

Perhaps the idea of "drawing a line" under The Beatles is futile, because their influence has never ceased to operate. All these years later, the world still belongs to John, Paul, George, and Ringo. We're just lucky to share it with them.

ABOVE The Fab Four in *Help!*: the band's promotional videos and feature films paved the way for music videos.

TOP The Beatles' mop-top haircuts (considered long at the time) were mocked by adults, but emulated by youngsters as an act of rebellion.

"THE BEATLES WILL GO ON AND ON . . . THE BEATLES EXIST WITHOUT US."

GEORGE HARRISON

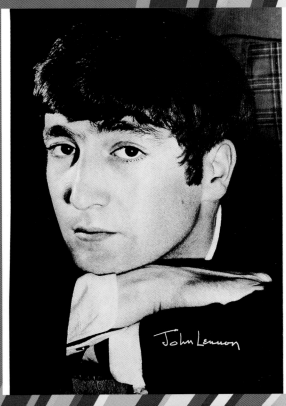

John Lennon

Paul McCartney

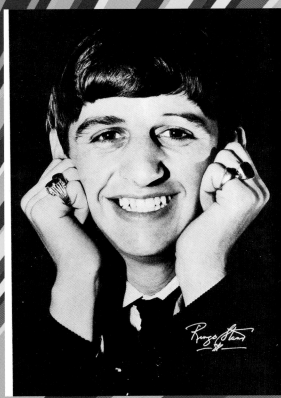

Ringo Starr

George Harrison